"First of all, I love a home cook! I am one and I learned from the best—my mom, Gwen. Second, the food looks amazing, and I can't wait to dive in! Last and most important, I love the whole vibe of this family: the love, the laughter, the lessons, the honesty. It's a beautiful, real snapshot into my friend Jen Hatmaker's life. Like the perfect dinner, you'll show up for the food, and you'll stay for the stories. Thanks for inviting me. Love, Trisha."

—TRISHA YEARWOOD, COUNTRY MUSIC LEGEND, HOST OF *TRISHA'S SOUTHERN KITCHEN*, AND FIVE-TIME COOKBOOK AUTHOR

"*Feed These People* puts people first, and then gives them a fantastic meal—and I'm 100 percent here for it! Jen celebrates the people around our tables. Trust me, you want Jen's cookbook!"

—MELISSA D'ARABIAN, AUTHOR OF *TASTING GRACE*

"*Feed These People* is absolutely stunning and makes me crave every recipe on every page. But more important, I echo Jen's heart and how it is filled by feeding the people she loves around her table."

—DANIELLE WALKER, BESTSELLING COOKBOOK AUTHOR AND WELLNESS EXPERT

"I'm in love with Jen's no-fuss, stress-free, and big-flavor approach to feeding her loved ones. With comforting recipes seasoned with Jen's trademark wit and humor, this book opens up like a warm hug and an invitation to her home kitchen!"

—MICHELLE TAM, *NEW YORK TIMES* BESTSELLING COOKBOOK AUTHOR AND CREATOR OF NOM NOM PALEO

Feed These People

Feed These

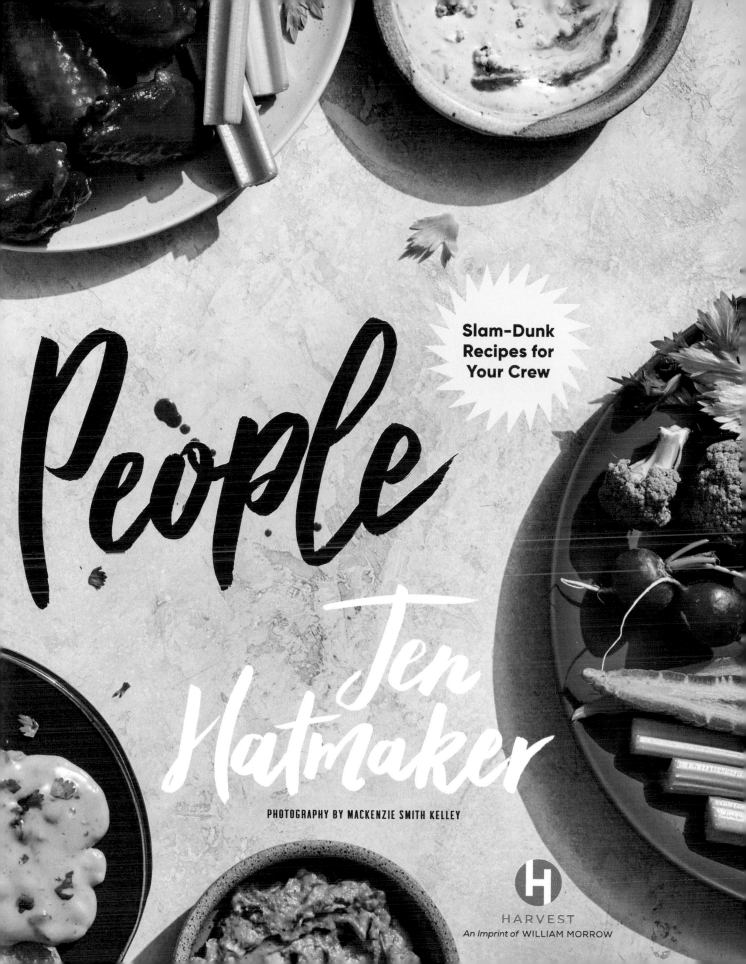

Slam-Dunk Recipes for Your Crew

People

Jen Hatmaker

PHOTOGRAPHY BY MACKENZIE SMITH KELLEY

HARVEST
An Imprint of WILLIAM MORROW

HarperCollins books may be purchased for educational,
business, or sales promotional use. For information, please email
the Special Markets Department at SPsales@harpercollins.com.

FIRST EDITION

Designed by Laura Palese
Photography © 2022 by Mackenzie Smith Kelley
Food styling by Maite Aizpurua
Prop styling by Taylor Cumbie
36 Gradients © Prime Dsgn via Creative Market

Library of Congress Cataloging-in-Publication
Data has been applied for.

ISBN 978-0-358-53914-8

22 23 24 25 26   RTL   10 9 8 7 6 5 4 3 2 1

FOR MY PEOPLE,

the greatest loves of my life.

I am the luckiest
girl in the world because
you are mine.

CONTENTS

FOOD FOR BREAKFAST
OR BRUNCH SO YOU CAN DRINK

FOOD FOR NOSHING
APPETIZERS & PARTY FOOD

FOOD FOR SPOONS
SAUCES & SOUPS

FOOD THAT GOES IN CARBS
SANDWICHES, SUBS & TACOS

INTRODUCTION

Look, sometimes life is weird and a girl named Jen Hatmaker ends up writing a cookbook. Is she a chef? She isn't. Does she have credentials? She doesn't. Did she go to culinary school? She didn't. Can she put down a double burger with mushrooms and onions and blue cheese sauce? She can, reader.

I'm just a home cook, and to secure that title, the best place to start is by being an eater.

So if you eat, you're in this club. Welcome.

I had no idea how to cook when I entered adulthood. Mom didn't teach us because we were a pain in the ass and who would want us in the kitchen? Plus, I grew up in the '80s and food sucked then. Or at least it did in Kansas. I don't know what the teens in New York were eating in 1988, but we were eating frozen Tyson chicken patties and Veg-All. The Cold War table was a real gauntlet.

I continued this race toward mediocrity in the kitchen until one day I had a six-year-old, a four-year-old, and a two-year-old and discovered this low-simmering rage toward their hunger, like a true psychopath—angry at preschoolers for wanting dinner again. That year on New Year's Day, not one to make resolutions because I already fail enough, thanks, I asked myself: "What is one thing I'd like to do *slightly* better this year?" (Take note, achievers.)

I answered myself: "Cooking. Because these jokers want to eat every day, apparently."

And just like that, I changed my mind about cooking. I decided to love it, on the spot. I decided to learn about garlic and red peppers and food that didn't come out of the freezer. I started watching the Food Network in the mid-2000s, and that became my culinary school. My instructors were Rachael Ray, Emeril, the Neelys, Paula Deen, Jamie Oliver, Nigella Lawson, Giada De Laurentiis, Sandra Lee. I purchased a grown-up person's knife. I bought cookbooks like I was single-handedly bankrolling the industry. I used ingredients I had never even seen, like ginger (WTH, ginger??).

To stop being resentful of kindergarteners, I decided to make the cooking hour delightful, so I asked myself, "What do you love?" Well, I love wine. I love *my* music instead of listening to freaking Barney. I love these babies, but I love them in another room

I'm just a home cook, and to secure that title, the best place to start is by being an eater.

Cooking wasn't the unmanageable beast I thought it was. It wasn't that precious. It wasn't that finicky. There were a million ways to dive in.

for a few hot minutes. So each night, having engineered an hour in the kitchen, I'd pour a glass of wine, play Norah Jones (2004, turn up!), and teach myself to cook.

Would you believe I grew to absolutely, positively love it? Not tolerate it, not endure it . . . love it. Cooking wasn't the unmanageable beast I thought it was. It wasn't that precious. It wasn't that finicky. There were a million ways to dive in. The "rules" were actually sparse. Teachers were abundant because of the World Wide Web. It was just food, with minimal consequences, so a recipe could go sideways four times before righting itself and no one would die. Cooking was a low-stakes creative outlet that resulted in homemade pizza and French onion soup, so there were no losers in this endeavor.

But the clear winner was me.

What an absolute joy cooking has become. This cookbook? My favorite project ever, and this is my *thirteenth* book, what in the whole earth. Combining a love of cooking with a love of writing and being obnoxious? Dream. Food and the table are so central to my happiness now.

A little note: This cookbook was just a tiny baby idea, barely formed but already titled, when I lost my twenty-six-year marriage. I hadn't written a single word yet, but feeding my family was the center point of the whole project. I called my agents and publisher with my raw, brokenhearted story and asked what to do with this failed project, this failed life.

They said, "Jen, do you still have children?"

"Yes. There are so many of them."

"Do you still have siblings?"

"Yes. We are so loud."

"Do you still have brothers-in-law and sisters-in-law and nieces and nephews?"

"Yes. Marrying into our wild family is a real ordeal."

"Do you still have parents?"

"Yes. They survived us."

"Do you still have best friends?"

"Yes. They are my life."

"Then feed these people. Get busy cooking."

But as surely as eating is the best prerequisite to being a cook, love is the only prerequisite to feeding the people.

We feed the people we love. That is the end of the formula. Some of them are married to us, some of them were born to us, some of them got stuck with us, some of them picked us. But as surely as eating is the best prerequisite to being a cook, love is the only prerequisite to feeding the people. I eat and I love; this project was never failed after all.

So welcome to this little weird place. Thanks for indulging my swears and whatever janky instructions I snuck past my editor, Stephanie. Def read all the stuff at the front of this book, which will help you make sense of the rest of it (allegedly). Don't you dare skip the vegetarian chapter; my pizza recipe is in that one, criminy. Enjoy the stories. They are only mildly exaggerated. Don't email me because I wrote "salt to taste" too much. Those pics? That is my house and those are my people, the North Star of my life.

Hope this little book helps you feed yours.

THE THING ABOUT COOKING . . .

I was a real Nervous Nellie when I first started cooking. Positive it was all utterly precise, I was married to recipes, distrustful of any (dormant) instincts I had, unwilling to adapt for my family's preferences, and constantly worried I was "getting it wrong." First of all, it is okay to be super crappy at something when you first start doing it, so never fear, new cooks. You can murder the crab cakes with lemon caper butter sauce at first, and who really cares. It's just food. Keep going.

But once I started cooking more, figuring out flavors and temps and combinations and ingredients, I moved solidly into the non-fussy category and never moved out. You'll for sure see that approach in the following pages, which some of you will love and others hate, but you already bought this cookbook, so it's too late, man.

Here are my main cooking philosophies:

 Trust yourself! You're a grown person with preferences, which you get to exercise with impunity. If you don't like cheddar cheese, sub in Monterey Jack. If you hate jalapeños, leave them out. Prefer it kickier? There's your cayenne. Want to use peaches instead of blueberries? It's a free damn country. I make a recipe exactly as written maybe one out of ten times. Most recipes are way more flexible than we think. TONS of the quantities I included can be increased or decreased, and you get to be in charge of your own dish. You really do. If you know for a fact that your family will not eat green chiles, then do the obvious thing: trade them in for a new family.

Taste and adjust. This is probably the number one way I got better as a home cook, and I wish I had a dime for every time I wrote this up in here. Recipes are not some mystery where you blindly stumble through eight steps and hope for the best. The difference between flat and perfect could be just one more teaspoon of salt, or one squeeze of lemon, or one little splash of vinegar—you just have to taste as you go. Taste each layer. Taste each stage. Adjust accordingly. No one needs to know you double dip the whole time. They're eating this food for free.

Fact: The first time you make a new recipe will be the longest it will ever take. Recipes feel most laborious when you have to keep reading instructions and sorting out steps and handling a new combination of ingredients. Second time? Way faster. Third time? You're absolutely nailing it. After long enough, you won't need the recipe anymore. Don't bail on an awesome dish because your first time through it was clunky. That second pass hits different.

Permanently retire the "Did I do this right?" thing. Most cooking isn't fussy or all that technical. It's as much poetry as prose. I wrote these recipes the way I like them, but that's because they paid me to. Here's your new approach: Taste it. Do you like it? Then you did it right. Don't overthink it. If technicality is super crucial, I'll tell you (like the Hot Honey on page 220, because if you get that wrong, your family is going to the ER).

Your kitchen, oven, stovetop, pans, burners, dishware, grill, altitude, and astrological sign all factor into temps and times. There are no two identical kitchens and, therefore, no two identical recipes. There is such a range of possibilities for any given set of steps. My oven cooks faster and hotter than every single recipe tells me it will. I 100% know to start checking my dish ten minutes earlier than suggested. This goes back to #1: trust yourself! If I told you it would take 25 minutes to bake, but at 19 minutes it's set and browned, then you win. If your nose, eyes, and touch tell you something different from what I wrote, you're becoming an intuitive cook! Your kitchen, your rules.

Finally, my best tip: Read each recipe from start to finish before you even grab your knife. Sometimes a step embedded later in the writing has info you'll want to know first. But mainly this gives you a real feel for what you're about to make. Of course, you'll deserve hazard pay for reading my recipes in their entirety because they're a mix of normal instructions and long, bossy, satirical commentary (it's a miracle this cookbook isn't 783 pages), but this step saves you time and wasted energy and gives you a solid sense of what the hell you're doing.

To aid this mental organizing, I broke each ingredient list into grouped steps. I learned this trick at Food Camp (you'll get to that; see my recipe for French Onion Soup on page 81) by just drawing a line between ingredients in order of when I would be using them. I put a line between steps so your lil' eyes can see what goes together and what's coming next.

FAVORITE KITCHEN TOOLS

Okay, campers, most of these recipes need caveman tools: fire and a pan. But there are a few kitchen tools you'll need or want that you may not have, not including stupid marketing scams like an "egg separator." Your egg separator is your hands (which are free). They really tried it.

Meat thermometer I'm not super precious about using this, because I generally use a fancy method called "cut into the center and look at it" or "touch it with my finger and feel it," but this is handy to have for some meats primarily so we don't give our families food poisoning.

Candy thermometer This is great for heating oil, which you're going to do a bunch up in this piece. Again, my method is "throw a pinch of flour in and see if it sizzles," but is it really hard to clip a candy thermometer to the pot and take the guesswork out?

Zester Lime and lemon zest are weird secret ingredients in a million recipes. Grated nutmeg is a weird secret ingredient in cream sauces. Grated garlic and ginger are sometimes the exact right tone. Just get one.

Cast-iron skillet You'll see my devotion shortly. Stovetop to oven, perfect crusty bottoms, I don't know, but you should have one. If you don't have your grandma's forty-five-year-old treasure, these are inexpensive and can be bought locally or online. Get one preseasoned, and for the love, read the instructions on upkeep.

Food scraper You use this thing to scoop up all your chopped ingredients and transfer them to your bowl or pan. IDK what it's actually called, but Sur La Table calls theirs a "food taxi," which I am now married to. You don't actually "have" to have one, but I love mine and use it every single day.

Dutch oven This is a large, heavy-duty enameled cast-iron pot and the home of half these recipes. About ten years ago, I ponied up $200 and bought a Staub Dutch oven, and by price per use, they owe me money now. This will last you for ten thousand years.

A really good knife This. This is the one. If you're going to invest in just one thing for your cooking journey, this is the one you pick. I will not tell another cook what knife to buy, because you have to love it in your hand, but go to a good store and hold twenty-five knives, cut their sample celery, ask 450 questions, and give them your money. Then keep that baby sharpened. This is your new pet. This is like your favorite child.

Blender and/or food processor I'm sure you have these. But you'll use both so many times in this book, I'd feel bad not saying it up front and making you mad later. I'm an Enneagram 3! I need you to like me! This is where my worth comes from!

Ramekins These are inexpensive and easy to find (including online), and you NEED them for French Onion Soup (page 81) and Crème Brûlée (page 246). They come in several sizes (doesn't really matter), but if you're debating sizes, get bigger ones to hold more soup, because only getting half a cup of French onion soup is devastating. If you're a big spender, get 8-ounce ramekins for soup and 4-ounce ramekins for crème brûlée. Or just do like I do and make crème brûlée in the big ones because you want a double portion. Plus, ramekins are adorable and can be used as cutesy little bowls for a million other things.

Everything else is basically normal kitchen stuff I'm assuming you have or can do without if you don't. But you have permission to buy whatever you want to use, and if someone fusses about it, they can cook their own damn food.

SOME STUFF TO KNOW . . .

My girlfriend Danielle Walker, cookbook author extraordinaire and all-around star, suggested recruiting a small army of volunteer recipe testers to run these through the gauntlet before turning them in to see what shakes out. *So much shook out.* God bless the testers who sent in eighty different versions of this question: "But how much salt really?"

Anyhow, some of what shook out included questions around unfamiliar ingredients, processes, products, and techniques. Let's knock these out.

How to peel ginger   I love fresh ginger, and there is no substitute. So this is a new thing you're going to learn because you care now too. Fresh ginger is sold in the produce section and looks like a tan, knobby root you pulled out of the ground, because that's what it is. You will never in a hundred years use the whole thing at once, but good news: it freezes perfectly. Most recipes call for 1 to 2 tablespoons of fresh ginger, which is about a 1-inch piece. Cut your fresh ginger into a bunch of 1-inch pieces and freeze them in an airtight baggie. When you need some, pop a piece in the microwave for 30 seconds, then peel it with a paring knife like a tiny little spicy potato. Ginger is fibrous and has to be grated or chopped and chopped into submission, but it is irreplaceable.

What to do with a leek   Leeks are like perfect little mild, tender onion cousins. They're soup's best friend. They love a pizza. They're also filthy and huge, but you end up using less than half of each one to make your food delicious. Cut off the root and most of the dark green tops. Once you have your leek trimmed down to the white and light green part, cut it in half lengthwise, right up the center. Place each half flat-side down and slice into half-moons. Scrumptious! Filthy! Scoop your leeks into a colander and rinse really well under cold running water. Use your hands to toss and dislodge the dirt and grit. Now you know about leeks.

Dredging This is an assembly line to fry things, so get excited. Fried things need either two or three coatings to get that nice crispy breaded exterior. Sometimes we need dry ▸ wet ▸ dry ▸ fry, but usually we just need wet ▸ dry ▸ fry. The "wet" is generally a beaten egg. The "dry" is some version of seasoned flour, bread crumbs (panko or otherwise), or ground nuts. Because my mom did, I always use pie plates for my dredging station. Put the egg in one pie plate, the dry in another, then, using one hand, dip your thing—let's say chicken—into the egg, coating all sides. Move the chicken to the dry station and use your other hand to dredge it (pro tip alert: this keeps your hand from becoming a clumpy breaded mess) until completely coated. Lay the breaded chicken in a single layer on a baking sheet until you're done dredging all your pieces, then slide them into your hot oil in batches. I give you measurements for dredging in the relevant recipes, but this is totally just whatever. If the dry station gets clumpy, just add more flour/bread crumbs/whatever to the pie plate. Throw away what you don't use. The only thing that matters is getting every piece totally coated. I love fried food. I love fried food as much as a teenage boy does.

What to do with whole lemongrass stalks I include lemongrass in two or three recipes, because it is the Thai secret to a certain flavor that just has to be lemongrass. First of all, your grocery store has fresh lemongrass! It looks like a single whitish stalk and is generally stocked by the herbs. To prep a stalk of lemongrass, turn your knife with the blunt side down like a hammer, sharp side up, and give the lemongrass several whacks on all sides. This is called bruising, and it prepares the lemongrass to release all its magic into your thing. Lemongrass is used for flavoring and usually gets fished out of the recipe at some point like a bay leaf.

Some other ingredients that you might not have, know, use, or think you like: You're going to try these because I'm telling you to:

+ **Sweet jalapeños:** Lord, the number of recipes I put these in. They're my favorite thing. They're just pickled sliced jalapeños but with more sugar in the brine. Like what bread-and-butter pickles are to dill pickles: same, but sweeter. These are also called candied jalapeños, bread-and-butter jalapeños, hot-and-sweet or sweet-and-hot jalapeños. Mt. Olive brand labels them "Sweet Heat." You can 100% get these on Amazon, and my favorite brand is Mrs. Renfro's.

+ **Fish sauce:** I don't want to hear it. It is required. One small bottle will last you a really long time, and a splash of it will turn your soups and sauces into magic. I won't tell you it's made of fermented anchovies, because you're going to make it weird but, trust me, it doesn't taste like it smells and it doesn't make your food taste like fish. If I call for it, I promise it makes the final result absolutely better.

+ **Curry paste:** This is a lazy cook's shortcut to Thai-inspired curry, and worth every penny. My favorite is red curry paste, but you can also buy green curry paste. OR BOTH. This lives in your fridge until it gets married to coconut milk and has a curry baby in under sixty seconds.

+ **Chipotle peppers in adobo sauce:** These are rehydrated smoked dried jalapeños that are canned in this delicious, spicy, tangy, tomato-y sauce. They're stocked in the canned foods aisle or Mexican foods section (if you live in Texas, this is half the store). They absolutely bring marinades and sauces to life. Spicy and smoky and hard to duplicate.

✦ **Chorizo:** Oh baby. Chorizo is spiced ground pork, and it is my life force. (I'm talking about Mexican chorizo here, which is fresh, not the cured Spanish version.) It is standard sausage kicked up. I use it constantly. You have two choices here: One, buy ground chorizo packaged in cellophane like ground beef (it's stocked in the meat department by the other pork stuff). Or two, buy chorizo in casings over by the sausage and hot dogs (just remove it from the casings before cooking it). But NEVER buy the horrid chorizo with eighteen weird ingredients sold in tubes. It will melt into nothingness over heat. Your chorizo ingredients should basically be pork, vinegar, spices, and salt. If you can't find it, you can use hot Italian sausage as an *okay* substitute.

✦ **Habanero peppers:** We're getting serious up in here. These are hotter than jalapeños but with a totally different flavor profile. They're little orange guys that suggest they might be sweet and mild like a yellow bell pepper, but that is a lie from the pit of hell. Throw on some kitchen gloves when you handle these so you don't accidentally touch your eye later and blind yourself. Habaneros have a delicious spicy, fruity flavor, and they're exactly right when they are called for. Don't freak out.

✦ **House Sauce:** I'm including a mention of my basic Italian red sauce because it's a staple ingredient in a dozen recipes. You can find the recipe on page 104 in the Food for Spoons chapter, so skip ahead and master this easy but perfect sauce. I kindly ask you to triple or quadruple the recipe, portion it, and freeze it so you have it on hand when you need it. If you obey me in this, you will want to make out with your make-and-freeze self.

WHO'S WHO IN THE BOOK

Say hello to the people who were kind enough to grace some of these pages.

✦ **Back on page 17 (and elsewhere), from left:** Caleb, Sydney, Gavin, Ben, and Remy Hatmaker

✦ **On this page, from left:** Drew, Calvin, Jana, Owen, and Sarah King

✦ **Page 202 and on the cover (in alphabetical order):** Andrew and Trina Barlow, Kim Devitt, Jackie Garrett, Jordan and Megan Hefferan, Larry and Jana King, Lindsay King, Scott and Lisa Vander Muelen, Tray and Jenny Pruet, Trace and Shonna Shelton, Rob and Anasofia Shelton, Mayson Shelton, Rob Walter, and Cortney Zager

1

FOOD *FOR* BREAKFAST

OR BRUNCH SO YOU CAN DRINK

JALAPEÑO
POLENTA AND CHORIZO BOWLS

SWAP
Ground hot Italian sausage for the chorizo.
Any cheese for the cheddar.

All my friends who (are forced to) read this cookbook will attest to this dish, because I have made it for every last one of them. It is this weird, decidedly Texan breakfast that people lose their minds over. This recipe never met an enemy except one guest who didn't like "cheddar, eggs, or avocados." I obviously asked him to leave immediately. He is dead to me now.

It looks suspect, it sounds strange, eaters aren't sure if they "like polenta" or "want sweet jalapeños at ten a.m.," but then they take one bite and start that happy humming sound people make when they love their bowl contents. Making brunch? Shove this into the hands of your people and become a stone-cold hero.

Fine, the polenta-versus-grits thing. This is a whole important deal in the South, so skip this paragraph if you couldn't care less. They're both made from ground corn, but traditionally from different types of corn, resulting in slightly different textures. They're both delicious and they're cooked the same, and everyone just needs to relax. I like polenta here for reasons I can't defend but will still argue about.

4 cups whole milk (don't hate)

1 cup stone-ground cornmeal

Salt and pepper

—

1 (12-ounce) package ground chorizo (please read my notes on chorizo on page 23)

3 tablespoons butter, plus more as needed

1 cup shredded cheddar cheese (4 ounces)

⅓ cup chopped sweet pickled jalapeños (sometimes called bread-and-butter jalapeños)

—

6 to 8 eggs (1 per serving)

Sliced avocado, for serving

// Heat the milk in a saucepan over medium heat (get it hot but don't let it boil). Whisk in the cornmeal ⅓ cup at a time. Add a good bit of salt and pepper. Whisk. And whisk. And whisk until the polenta turns thick and fabulous, about 10 minutes.

// Meanwhile, in a skillet on the next burner over, brown your chorizo (just like cooking ground beef)—this takes 6 to 8 minutes, and I always drain it before serving, because chorizo has tons of very, very delicious fat that renders off. CHORIZO IS LIFE. I'm so sad for anyone who doesn't know what chorizo is. It's everything you've ever wanted, is what it is.

RECIPE CONTINUES

// Once your polenta is nice and thick and creamy (similar to the consistency of mashed potatoes), pull it off the heat and stir in the butter, cheese, jalapeños, and salt and pepper to taste. Stir until it's all melted and mixed. Eat four quick spoonfuls because you are a human being with needs, and creamy cheesy polenta will meet needs you didn't even know you had.

// Recruit a helper to make fried eggs. Beautiful eggs cracked into tons of butter in a pan over medium-low heat. Cook for 2 minutes on the first side, flip, and cook for 2 more minutes. Salt and pepper like your life depends on it.

// Plate everything up in a cute bowl, one per person:

// Creamy, cheesy polenta on the bottom.

// Then a scoop of spicy, delicious chorizo.

// A yummy fried egg, over easy or over medium. (Or poached, if you love that.)

// Sliced avocado, to top it off.

// Serve with mimosas and jazz on the speakers, and collect your praise, because whoever you invited over for brunch just became your new best friends. BECAUSE THIS BREAKFAST IS HARD-CORE LEGIT.

Note

LEFTOVER POLENTA?

Pour it into a small square baking dish, cover, and refrigerate overnight. Next day, cut it into squares, dust with flour, and sear in a hot pan in 2 tablespoons oil. Top with a fried egg. Polenta cakes!

Black Pepper Biscuits

The fun thing about making biscuits from scratch is that you can just think the thought "I bet hot, fluffy biscuits with butter would be delicious" and be eating them 30 minutes later. The other fun thing is that you don't have to buy anything because you for sure have biscuit makin's on hand. And yes, you do have buttermilk—just see my note on page 33.

Whoever thinks homemade biscuits are hard hasn't made them. Our grandmas made them because they cost around 12 cents and require barely any ingredients. **Do you have hands? Then you can make biscuits.**

12 tablespoons (1½ sticks) cold salted butter, cut into small pieces, plus more for greasing

4 cups flour

4 teaspoons baking powder

1 teaspoon baking soda

1 teaspoon salt

—

1½ cups cold buttermilk

—

½ cup heavy cream or half-and-half

Freshly cracked black pepper

—

2 tablespoons butter, melted, for brushing

// Preheat your oven to 425°F and butter a baking sheet.

// In a large bowl, whisk together the flour, baking powder, baking soda, and salt, then add the pieces of butter. If you are a serious baker, which I am decidedly not, you probably have a pastry cutter. If you're like me and barely bake because your idea of dessert is chips, then cut your butter into the flour by taking two knives and slicing back and forth through all those little butter pieces like Edward Scissorhands until it looks like cornmeal. You can also just do this with your hands like the pilgrims did.

// Add your buttermilk and mix with a spatula until the dough just comes together. Turn it out onto a floured surface and start working it together. Yes, it is so freaking sticky. WHY, BISCUIT DOUGH? It's supposed to be like that, but my gosh. If you keep your hands cool and damp with cold water, it helps a little. Basically just work it until it comes together (which takes less than 1 minute, so my drama here is definitely unwarranted) and form it into a big square about an inch thick. You should still see little chunks of butter in there, and that is how we know Jesus loves us. If you specialize in math, you might realize you've put 12 tablespoons of butter into dough that makes 12 biscuits. Plus, we're going to brush them with melted butter later and also slather them with some more on the inside before we eat them. WE DON'T CARE, BUTTER HATERS. Our moms fed us Country Crock our whole childhoods and we're making up for lost time.

RECIPE CONTINUES

// I like to cut the dough into 12 squares. Sure, you could cut them out with a round cutter, or you could just cut square biscuits with no leftover dough and be done with it. That last sad biscuit made from the orphaned dough is always a hot mess, and you know it.

// Transfer the biscuits to your buttered baking sheet and brush the tops with the cream. I like to crack just the barest bit of black pepper over them because I already told you I'm not a sweet pastry person and I just put pepper on my biscuits so now you know I mean business.

// Bake on the middle rack for 12 to 15 minutes, until the biscuits are puffy and golden. Then brush the tops with the melted butter because no one tells you how to live.

// Please, for the love, eat these while they're hot and slather them, I mean SLATHER them, with even more butter on the inside. Obviously, add delicious honey or marmalade. OR, omg, fry thick slices of ham and make a breakfast biscuit sandwich with a slice of Swiss and some honey mustard.

// Summary: A buttered pan, butter in the dough, butter brushed on top, butter on the inside. Thank you for coming to my TED Talk.

Note

Homemade "buttermilk" is just regular milk with some vinegar in it (1½ cups milk + 1 tablespoon distilled white vinegar). I went back to my laundry room where my vinegar has been trying to get the weird smell out of my front-loading washing machine and put a tablespoon in my milk. And that is the story of how I made buttermilk.

GINGERBREAD SPICE
Dutch Baby

SERVE WITH
sliced bananas, berries, whipped cream, Nutella, and/ or flavored syrup.

This recipe 100% belongs in the Food for When You Want to Seem Fancy chapter, but it's a brunch star, so here we are. The only confusing thing about this dish is why it's called a Dutch baby, which is a little dark and reminiscent of a Grimms' fairy tale: *"And this is where we roast the children."*

Anyway, sorry if I've now made this weird for you, because a Dutch baby is so delicious and fun to serve. It gently suggests to your guests that you know a damn thing or two in the kitchen, when what you really know how to do? Is make a pancake. A Dutch baby is just a fancy pancake with the star power of a popover and the elegance of a crepe, and it doesn't matter if you don't know how to make either of those because you're about to. Look at you, knowing new things.

This comes together before your oven is barely warm, which is why this is a great second dish for brunch—it takes virtually no time while you're making your savory breakfast scramble and/or drinking mimosas and/or drinking Bloody Marys and/or drinking Bellinis.

BATTER

½ cup flour

¾ cup milk

2 teaspoons ground ginger

1 teaspoon ground cinnamon

½ teaspoon ground nutmeg

3 eggs

Pinch of salt

THE REST OF IT

3 tablespoons butter

Powdered sugar, for dusting

Maple syrup, for serving

// A preheated pan is the most important part, so before you even grab your flour, turn your oven to 400°F and throw your cast-iron skillet in. (Or any oven-safe skillet, as long as it's 9 or 10 inches in diameter, but I revere cast iron for reasons that are ambiguous yet very, very inflexible.)

// **Make the batter:** Combine the batter ingredients and whisk and whisk until perfectly smooth. If you have angry feelings about whisking, throw it all in your blender. And now that's done. (See what I'm saying? Your oven has been on for 3 minutes.) The good news is that this batter is in peak form if you let it sit for 15 minutes or so. The flour absorbs the liquids and the texture turns out super dreamy.

RECIPE CONTINUES

// So do something else for 10 or 15 minutes.

// **Now for the rest of it:** Carefully take your preheated skillet out of the oven and drop in the butter. Yes, this is a lot of butter, and no, I am not sorry. Swirl it around so it coats the sides of the pan, then pour your batter right in. I hate myself for even saying this, but if you pour the batter in in a figure-eight pattern, it makes pretty ridges when it bakes. I DON'T MAKE THE RULES, OKAY? This will not look impressive yet and you will be tempted to doubt me, but *you would be wrong, Janice.*

// Back into the hot oven. Set a timer for 15 minutes and also use your nose. This may need up to 20 minutes. When it smells like a gingerbread factory and is all puffed and brown and crinkled on the edges, it's ready. Can you even believe how gorgeous it looks?? This is the brunch business.

// If you used a charming cast-iron skillet (see previous declaration), you can serve this right out of the pan as long as you put a cute tea towel around the handle so your guests don't go home with third-degree burns. The Dutch baby itself isn't sweet, but dust the whole thing with powdered sugar and set some warm maple syrup out in a sweet little pouring pitcher, and it's the perfect balance.

// If you're just serving your Dutch baby on a Saturday morning to delight your kids, it'll feed three or four people. If it's one brunch dish out of several? You can cut it into wedges and feed a few more. You can also easily double the recipe and bake two batches. If you serve this with brown sugar and black pepper bacon, I'm coming over.

Notes

Add 1 teaspoon vanilla extract and 1 tablespoon sugar instead of the warm spices.

Arrange fruits like blueberries, raspberries, or sliced peaches over the bottom of the skillet and then pour the batter over top. (Scattering fruit on top of the batter will keep the Dutch baby from rising as impressively.)

Latkes

with Rosemary Sour Cream

Recently, my girlfriend asked, "What are your top three favorite foods?" and without really thinking hard or missing a beat, I answered, "Hash browns, french fries, and chips." She looked at me quietly for a moment and said, "Did you just list three fried potato products?" APPARENTLY SO, SARAH. And for the record, the perfect hash browns are shredded and come straight off the greasiest fifty-year-old griddle at the sketchiest diner you can find, and if you don't agree, come fight me.

Enter latkes, the Jewish crispy oniony fried potato cakes traditionally served during Hanukkah (although this Texas Christian is here for them all year long).

4 russet potatoes (about 2 pounds), peeled	1 cup high-temp oil (like grapeseed or canola)
1 onion, chopped	Sea salt, for sprinkling
—	—
2 eggs, lightly beaten	1 cup sour cream
½ cup flour	1 tablespoon chopped fresh rosemary
1 tablespoon salt	
Pepper	

Note

If you have any leftovers, tomorrow morning they should go into breakfast tacos or be layered in a breakfast sandwich with a fried egg and crispy bacon or sausage.

// Preheat your oven to 250°F and stick a wire rack on a rimmed baking sheet.

// A well-known fact about me is that I hate to hand-grate things. Cheese, potatoes, I don't care. It is my least favorite kitchen chore. This is melodramatic and unreasonable, yet here we are. I will 100% use my food processor to shred stuff. Yes, I would rather clean its fourteen separate parts than hand-grate one ounce of food. Thank you for letting me live. So hand grate your potatoes if you hate yourself (or if you must). Otherwise, use your food processor's grating disc.

// Throw your shredded potatoes into a large bowl filled with cold water, let them soak for about 3 minutes, then drain in a colander. Wrap the potatoes and onion in a clean kitchen towel and wring out as much moisture as possible. Otherwise, your latkes will be too wet and won't hold together or crisp up, and Hanukkah is ruined.

// Dry off that large bowl, throw in the potatoes, onion, eggs, flour, and salt, season with pepper, and mix.

// Heat ¼ cup of the oil in a skillet over medium-high heat until a pinch of flour thrown in sizzles on contact. Spoon about 2 tablespoons of the latke mix into the hot oil for each latke and flatten them out a bit with your spatula. You should be able to fit four or five latkes in each batch. Let them cook for 4 to 5 minutes, until the bottoms are delicious, crunchy brown, then carefully flip them and fry on the second side for 4 to 5 minutes. Transfer this batch to the wire rack on the baking sheet, sprinkle with sea salt, and keep warm in the oven while you finish the other batches like a boss. Between batches, scoop out any darkened fried bits that got away from their mother and add more oil as needed.

// Traditionally, latkes are served with sour cream and applesauce. But applesauce doesn't work with my fried potato theology. (I was at brunch with my girlfriends when my friend Jenny reported a group of Midwesterners on social media saying their favorite add-in for chili was cinnamon rolls, and we blankly stared at her for three minutes.) (I just googled "is chili and cinnamon rolls a thing?" in case Jenny was full of crap, and IT IS. Blasphemy!)

// My point is that some things seem weird together to me, and applesauce and fried potatoes are one of them. I'm sorry, Jesus! But may I introduce you, reader, to the wonder of latkes and rosemary sour cream?? Just mix the sour cream and rosemary and dollop on your hot, crispy latkes. Omg. Just omg. I want to eat these every day of my damn life.

Frittata Casserole

I don't know if a "frittata casserole" is a real thing, but I was playing too fast and loose with the pure version of a frittata, so I added the word "casserole" to atone for my indiscretions. Kind of how Southern women add the phrase "bless her heart" to the end of a scathing, sick burn to soften the blow: "In that unfortunate sweater ensemble, Mary Kate looks like a beached whale that rolled up on the Pensacola shores, bless her heart."

Make sure you have what you need for a frittata. And what that means is whatever you have, plus eggs and cream. Yay! Frittatas are a breakfast dumping ground for leftovers, which, if you're like me, looks like eight to fourteen small containers, baggies, and sloppily wrapped dishes in my fridge at all times. I'll save four bites of leftovers like I'm a survivor of the Great Depression, which drives my family crazy until my small Tupperware of leftover caramelized onions makes their frittata casserole delicious, so who's laughing now, jokers?

2 cups ground sage sausage (or chorizo, or ground turkey, or seriously? Any meat. Any leftovers.)

1 tablespoon olive oil

1 tablespoon butter

½ onion, diced

1 green bell pepper, diced

2 garlic cloves, chopped

1 cup halved cherry tomatoes

Leftover carbs (see Note; optional)

8 large eggs

1 cup half-and-half (or heavy cream!)

Tons of salt and pepper

1 cup shredded cheese (I had Gruyère, but all cheese is good cheese; 4 ounces)

FOR SERVING (OPTIONAL)

Sour cream

Salsa

// Preheat your oven to 400°F.

// In your 10-inch cast-iron skillet (or any similar oven-safe skillet), brown the sausage over medium heat for 6 to 8 minutes, then remove it with a slotted spoon and transfer to a plate. (If you're using leftovers, just warm them through and transfer to a plate.) Add the oil and butter to that yummy fat in the skillet, then add the onion, bell pepper, garlic, and tomatoes and sauté for 7 to 8 minutes, until the veggies have softened.

// In a separate bowl, whisk your eggs and cream with S&P. Yuuuuuummy. Stir in the cheese.

// **Note:** The reason I'm calling this a casserole is because if I have it, I press any leftover carbs I have on hand into the bottom of my cast-iron like a crust. And I do mean "any"—leftover mashed potatoes, rice, grits, risotto, cornbread, hash browns, whatever. If you don't have anything, skip this, because we aren't making mashed potatoes at nine a.m. I'm also calling this a casserole because "whatever you have" and "all cheese is good cheese" and "any meat" is a sloppy recipe at best, bless its heart.

RECIPE CONTINUES

// So if you have leftover carby-carbs, transfer the sautéed veggies to the same plate as the meat, throw some more butter into the cast iron to melt (yes, we're still using the same skillet), then press your carbs into the bottom of the pan. Spread the sausage (or whatever meat) and the veggies over the crust, then pour the eggs over the whole thing. Let it sit on the burner for a minute or two, until the edges just start to set. Then stick it in the oven for 15 minutes or so, until a knife stuck in the middle comes out clean. Let it cool for 5 to 10 minutes before serving.

// I love to dollop on sour cream and salsa, because I apparently like to front-load my dairy. And since you're cleaning out your fridge, chop up whatever fruit is about to go, sprinkle with sugar, and toss, and now you have "fruit salad" to go with your "frittata casserole" like a real champion who makes up food names.

Remember, a frittata is just eggs, cream, and cheese poured over any stuff and baked. My frittata combo is always: whatever is in a baggie or Tupperware container in my fridge. The end. Good frittata combos:

- **Ham and Swiss, 1 tablespoon Dijon mustard whisked into the eggs**
- **Onion, tons of fresh herbs (any and all), Parmesan**
- **Ham, asparagus, Gruyère**
- **Spinach, olives, feta**
- **Basil, tomatoes (or sun-dried tomatoes), mozzarella**
- **Mushrooms, bacon, thyme, Swiss**
- **Onions, green chiles, sriracha, cheddar**
- **Scallions, cilantro, queso fresco**
- **Roasted red peppers, artichokes, goat cheese**
- **Sausage, pepperoni, green bell peppers, ricotta**
- **Broccoli, ham, Parmesan**
- **Chorizo, potatoes, cheddar**

BLUEBERRY ALMOND

French Toast Bake

My girlfriends say this is their favorite recipe in the cookbook, but that's because I never give them sweet food so they're just overresponding. (One time my son Caleb spent the night at a friend's house, and he came home and said, "Mom! They had dessert! For no reason!" We have dessert on birthdays and the Fourth of July, and that's only because my mom or sister-in-law brings it.)

This is as not-sweet as I could get a sweet breakfast recipe, and it is diviiiiine. My friends, while melodramatic, are not wrong. Also, this has to sit overnight before baking, so it's the perfect breakfast on Christmas morning or for brunch when you don't want to be in the weeds, because all you have to do the next day is make a quick crumble and pop this in the oven. This is no fail, and you have most of the ingredients already. There is not a living being who wouldn't love this.

Butter, for greasing

1 loaf French bread (one or two days old), cut into 1-inch cubes

1 pint fresh blueberries

6 ounces mascarpone cheese

—

8 eggs

3 cups heavy cream

3 tablespoons sugar

1 teaspoon vanilla extract (or a splash more—live your life)

½ teaspoon almond extract

1 teaspoon ground cinnamon

½ teaspoon grated nutmeg (freshly grated if you have it!)

Pinch of salt

ALMOND CRUMBLE

6 tablespoons (¾ stick) butter, melted

1 cup packed brown sugar

1 cup sliced almonds

FOR SERVING

Powdered sugar

Maple syrup

// **The night before serving:** Butter a 9 x 13-inch baking dish and toss in half the bread cubes. Scatter the blueberries evenly on top. (Not blueberry season? This fruit is flexible. Use whatever is ripe. This is great with peaches, any berries, even chopped apples in the fall.) Dollop the mascarpone all over, which is an Italian sweet cream cheese we all need in our lives. Top with the rest of the bread cubes. You've created a fruity, creamy middle section that's a REAL NICE SURPRISE.

// From the ingredient list, whisk together the "eggs through pinch of salt" in a bowl until totally mixed, then pour it evenly over the casserole. (Fun fact: There is only ½ teaspoon of almond extract in here, but it's the first thing you taste when this is done, and it is irreplaceable. Don't skip it!) Cover the dish with foil and pop it in the fridge overnight. The custard soaks into the bread, and you'll just not believe it.

// **The next morning:** Preheat your oven to 350°F.

// Take the French toast out of the fridge to take the chill off while you put the crumble together, which just means combining the melted butter, brown sugar, and almonds in a bowl. (The sliced almonds are my favorite part of this recipe, but my mom likes slivered almonds instead, because they are "less assertive," a preference I would expect out of an Enneagram 9. But this Enneagram 3 asserts the hell out of those almonds. Big crunch! Big flavor! Big pieces! Big energy!) Spread the crumble evenly over the top of the French toast.

// Bake this for around 45 minutes, until the casserole is toasty and brown on top. Let it rest for 10 minutes before slicing into it. Dust the whole French toast bake with powdered sugar and serve with maple syrup. Don't let your friends cut their own servings or they'll eat the whole pan.

PEACH CORN CAKES

SWAP blueberries for the peaches.

My girlfriend Jenny calls pancakes "breakfast dessert," and she regularly orders one à la carte *in addition to* her main breakfast at restaurants. For dessert. Although I reach for savory breakfast most times, sometimes a pancake just HITS. I can get swept up in breakfast dessert mania too, because I am an American with rights.

When my upstairs is overrun by my teenagers and their friends (see: all the times), and everyone is sleeping helter-skelter up there on a Friday night, Saturday morning calls for a giant batch of pancakes. They're basically free to make, I always have all the ingredients, and they can feed boys who never get full.

Why do the teen boys never get full? Who can explain this to me? Why do they eat first and second dinner, late-night dinner, first breakfast, and also breakfast dessert? I always said "Feed them and they will come" because I wanted to be the teen house, and I did, and they came, and this is the story of why I make twenty pounds of Saturday-morning pancakes and keep a Costco-size bag of disgusting pepperoni rolls in my freezer, and by disgusting, I mean delicious.

Peach corn cakes are a delightful twist on the usual suspects and the perfect summer breakfast when peaches are too divine for words. This recipe makes a normal person's quantity, but if you're feeding seven to ten hungry teens, double or triple it. Worst-case scenario: You freeze the leftovers for later. There will be no leftovers. Forget I wrote that sentence.

Corn cakes + syrup + coffee alone makes this recipe worth it, but add the fresh peaches, and every bite is pure joy. I recognize that summer peaches are a Texas treasure because that is a thing we grow. Every self-respecting Texan has pulled off the road to buy a bag of peaches from the back of some farmer's truck in July. It's a state crime not to. Look it up. If your region doesn't include groves and groves of peach trees, your grocery store will oblige your needs, but you should consider moving to Texas for the sake of your peach corn cakes.

¾ cup flour

¾ cup coarse yellow cornmeal

2 tablespoons sugar

1 teaspoon baking powder

½ teaspoon baking soda

½ teaspoon salt

—

1¼ cups buttermilk (see Note, page 33)

3 tablespoons butter, melted

2 eggs

1 teaspoon vanilla extract (I will not be mad if you fudge this higher)

Butter, for grilling

—

2 cups diced peeled fresh ripe peaches

Butter, for serving

Warm maple syrup, for serving

// In a large bowl, whisk together the flour, cornmeal, sugar, baking powder, baking soda, and salt. In a separate bowl, whisk the buttermilk, melted butter, eggs, and vanilla until totally combined. Add the wet ingredients to the dry ones, and whisk until smooth and gorgeous. Add a cup or so of the diced peaches to the batter and stir to combine. Save the rest for topping, because pancake decorations are pretty.

// Corn cakes love butter with all their heart. Think of how much cornbread loves butter, and now you understand its needs. So onto a hot griddle, add a bunch of butter to fry these in. There is no quantity except "a lot" so just work that out. Ladle ¼ cup of the batter for each corn cake onto the griddle, and flip when it is bubbly on top and nice and brown on the bottom, 3 to 4 minutes. Fry on the other side for another couple of minutes until browned, and keep the corn cakes in a warm oven until you're through all the batches. Or transfer them directly onto the plates the teen boys are standing there holding.

// Top with a little scoop of the fresh peaches and some warm maple syrup. Do I add additional butter on top? I do. The surprising bite of warm peaches inside the crunch of the corn cake batter? I'd order this as breakfast *and* breakfast dessert 100 times out of 100.

Texas Migas

In 1998, when I was twenty-four, we moved to Texas and my eating world was turned upside down. Exhibit A: La Paletera was on every solitary corner, and its specialty was a giant cup of diced fruit doused with chili-lime Tajín seasoning. Chili powder! On fruit! Exhibit B: Barbacoa tacos. I ate my first one exactly as the ancestors intended, with pit-roasted shredded beef cheeks, chopped onion, and cilantro, and reader, I saw stars. Exhibit C: Tamales. I'd never even heard of them. Ate some at a Christmas party, handmade by the aunts and grandmas the entire previous day, and rededicated my life to Jesus on the spot.

Texas, my Texas! All my babies were born and raised here, so they basically got pureed tamales in their bottles. They never knew anything different from the magic cuisine in this over-the-top state.

Which brings me to exhibit D: migas. I remember where I was sitting the first time I ate this perfect Mexican breakfast. I had no idea you could put all that in your eggs. Happily, in Texas we'll add onions and peppers and fried tortillas to our eggs if we damn well want to. We'll put it on our menus and feed it to our babies and act like that's the proper way to eat eggs, WHICH IT IS. If I had to pick, I'd say this is my favorite breakfast of all time.

2 tablespoons oil

1 tablespoon butter

5 corn tortillas (gotta be corn), cut into ½-inch-wide strips, then into 2-inch pieces

___

1 small onion, diced

1 green bell pepper, diced

2 jalapeños, seeded and diced

2 Roma (plum) tomatoes, diced

2 garlic cloves, diced

___

8 eggs

3 tablespoons heavy cream or milk

Salt and pepper

1 tablespoon butter

___

2 cups shredded Monterey Jack or pepper Jack cheese (8 ounces) (no one will be mad if you add more cheese)

1 cup chopped fresh cilantro

___

Sliced avocado, for serving

COULD ALSO SERVE WITH . . .

Refried beans

Salsa

Cotija cheese, sprinkled on top

Pico de gallo

Sliced jalapeños (live on the edge!)

Tortillas, for wrapping the migas

// You're going to fry those tortilla strips first, but don't panic. It takes 5 minutes. In a skillet, heat the oil and butter over medium-high. Add the tortilla strips and cook, stirring, until they're crispy and brown all over, around 5 minutes. Remove with a slotted spoon and transfer to a paper towel–lined plate to drain.

// Add the onion, bell pepper, and jalapeños to the skillet and cook, stirring frequently, until they're softened, about 5 minutes.

// Meanwhile, in a bowl, whisk together the eggs, cream, and salt and pepper until fluffy and light.

// Turn the heat under the skillet down to medium-low, add the tomatoes and garlic, and cook for 1 more minute. (I don't like the tomatoes to get mushy, so just warm them through here.) Add the butter to the skillet, then pour in the eggs and gently push them around the pan with a spatula. You want these eggs barely cooked through, still a little glossy, and definitely soft. NO BROWN. Brown eggs make me cry all the tears in Austin.

// Add the fried tortilla strips, cheese, and cilantro and stir to combine, then take it off the heat. I am just saying that if you tuck a dollop of refried beans and a scoop of migas inside a warm tortilla and top it with sliced avocado and salsa, you're never going to eat anything else for the rest of your living days.

SHAKSHUKA

Peppery tomato sauce and eggs-over-easy got married and had a baby named shakshuka. It was born in North Africa, traveled around the Middle East, then immigrated to the United States, where Americans went facedown into its rich, tomato-y goodness like wild animals. The first time I ate shakshuka in a restaurant, I kept looking around to see if anyone was bearing witness to my Special Important Moment. Eggs? In spicy tomato sauce? With crusty bread?? Thank you, Egypt! Thank you, Israel! Thank you, chickens!

This is a one-skillet breakfast/brunch dish, but because it's so hearty and filling, shakshuka is a lead contender for breakfast-for-dinner. There are tons of variations, but this is a classic recipe (sort of), and I'll tell you straight up that you'll love it.

3 tablespoons olive oil

1 onion, chopped

1 red bell pepper, chopped

Salt and black pepper

—

3 garlic cloves, chopped

1 teaspoon ground cumin

1 teaspoon paprika

1 teaspoon chili powder

½ teaspoon cayenne pepper

—

1 (28-ounce) can crushed tomatoes (fire-roasted, if you're wild like that)

1 tablespoon sugar

—

1 cup crumbled fresh goat cheese (or feta!)

6 to 8 eggs (1 per serving)

FOR SERVING

Handful of fresh cilantro, chopped

Crusty French bread, toasted and buttered

Hot sauce (optional)

// In a cast-iron skillet (or other oven-safe skillet), heat the olive oil over medium heat. Add the onion and bell pepper, sprinkle with salt and black pepper, and sauté until nice and soft. I don't like these crunchy in the sauce, so I let them go around 15 minutes.

// Add the garlic, cumin, paprika, chili powder, and cayenne and stir until fragrant and incorporated, around 2 minutes.

// Time to preheat your oven to 375°F.

// Pour in the tomatoes and sugar, season with salt and black pepper, and let the sauce simmer until it thickens up. (Fine, the sugar isn't traditional and isn't in a shakshuka recipe anywhere, but canned tomatoes are so acidic, the sugar balances the flavor to my exact liking. It's just 1 tablespoon! Everyone calm down.) This really needs to simmer for at least 20 minutes. Tomato sauce just does. It'll taste too sharp if you pull it too soon. In fact, don't even taste it for 20 minutes.

// *However*, at the 20-minute mark, it is time to taste and adjust. Depending on a million factors, you may need more salt or sugar or even a few more minutes on the heat. Cooking is never as formulaic as cookbooks make it seem. Trust yourself! Trust your mouth! If you want sugar in your shakshuka, you shall have it!

// When the sauce is just perfect for you, sprinkle the goat cheese all over. Then make 6 to 8 wells in the sauce, evenly spaced around the skillet, and carefully crack an egg into each one. Sprinkle each egg with salt and black pepper, slide the whole thing into the oven, and bake until your eggs are just set but still over easy or over medium, 6 to 8 minutes. You want the whites totally opaque but the yolks still a little jiggly (this is a technical term).

// Sprinkle the cilantro over the whole skillet and serve the saucy eggs in shallow bowls with hunks of buttered toasted crusty bread. Trust me, you want to sop that sauce up, and sturdy bread is the man for the job. We drizzle ours with hot sauce too, because we have no chill.

NOTE

HAVE LEFTOVER SAUCE?

It's delicious the next morning spooned over creamy grits or polenta.

2

FOOD *FOR* NOSHING

APPETIZERS & PARTY FOOD

Dip Dinner Hummus

I pulled this term out of my ass one year when the kids were little and I wasn't in the mood to beg them to eat like some pathetic lady shilling to kindergarteners. Thus, Dip Dinner was born, as kids will eat anything with a dipping sauce because they are suckers. Also, it's super novel to make one huge board of Things to Dip plus Dips to Dip the Things In and let everyone gather around it and eat like cavemen. This counts as dinner because we say it does.

This hummus is a staple dip, and every single cracker, crostini, chip, or veggie on earth can get dunked into it with impunity. Your bases are officially covered.

Cook's note: I made around fifty batches of mediocre hummus until I stumbled on the tip of the century from Kathryne Taylor (of *Cookie and Kate* blog fame). She, in turn, stumbled on this tip from Israeli chef Michael Solomonov, who is evidently the Kingpin World Champion of hummus. So what I'm saying is that someone on the internet has already solved your recipe problem, and if you include their tips in your cookbook, you need to send them a quarter every time someone makes this and raves about it. Kate and Michael, send me your Venmo accounts. You are about to receive tens of dollars.

Feeding a group? Want leftovers tomorrow? Double this and thank yourself later.

¼ cup fresh lemon juice

2 garlic cloves, chopped

1 teaspoon kosher salt

___

1 (15-ounce) can chickpeas, drained and rinsed

½ teaspoon baking soda

___

⅓ cup tahini

½ teaspoon ground cumin

¼ cup extra-virgin olive oil, plus more for drizzling

GARNISH OPTIONS

Chopped fresh parsley or chives

Everything bagel seasoning blend

Paprika

// In a small bowl, combine the lemon juice, garlic, and salt. Set this aside to mellow out a smidge before you add it to the rest of this magic.

// The problem with just dumping the chickpeas into your food processor straight out of the can is that they don't break down enough no matter how long you blend them. They end up gritty, and the Number One Rule of hummus is utter, total creaminess. So thanks to Michael and Kate, now we know what to do (because we sure as hell aren't going to soak and peel them): Put the chickpeas in a saucepan, add the baking soda, cover with several inches of water, bring to a boil over high heat, lower to medium, and boil for 20 minutes. This is the secret to life. It breaks down both the chickpeas and their skins so they can be blended into creamy perfection. What does the baking soda do? I don't know because I'm not a scientist, but I've done this with and without, and I am telling you the baking soda is important. Just add it.

// Drain the chickpeas in a fine-mesh strainer and run cold water over the whole mushy pile. Mushy chickpeas! Now we're cooking with gas!

// In your food processor, zip up the garlic and lemon juice. Add the tahini and process until blended and creamy. Scrape down the sides of the processor bowl and add the cumin and chickpeas (if you're using any flavor add-ins, throw them in now). With the motor running, drizzle in the olive oil. Oh my my my my. Give it a little taste and see if you'd like to add anything. You might want a hair more salt; if it's too thick for your liking, you can add a tablespoon or two of cold water. Transfer to a bowl, drizzle with olive oil, and sprinkle with whatever hummus decorations you want. It is sooooooo gorgeous and sooooooo creamy and sooooooo yummy. Add some store-bought salsa and quick guacamole, and Dip Dinner is served.

Hummus variations

- ✦ **Add one bulb roasted garlic**
- ✦ **Add pitted olives**
- ✦ **Add roasted red peppers**
- ✦ **Add pickled jalapeños**
- ✦ **Add sun-dried tomatoes**

Other dips to add to Dip Dinner

- ✦ **Fresh salsa**
- ✦ **Chunky guacamole**
- ✦ **Spicy Ranch (page 98)**

Dip Dinner
Hummus
54

Pimento Cheese

with Candied Jalapeños

8 ounces sharp cheddar cheese (in a block, not preshredded)

8 ounces Monterey Jack (or Colby, or Fontina, or Gruyère) cheese

1 (6-ounce) jar roasted red peppers, drained and diced (most jars are 12 ounces, in which case, use half!)

⅓ cup sweet pickled jalapeños, diced

¼ to ½ cup mayo (you know my policy: real mayo only)

¼ to ½ cup plain Greek yogurt (a new policy to know about me: full-fat only)

1 tablespoon Dijon mustard

1 (4-ounce) jar chopped pimentos, drained

1 teaspoon salt

1 teaspoon black pepper

2 to 3 dashes cayenne pepper, to taste (optional)

I am famous for this pimento cheese, and honestly? I've never been prouder. You can keep your accolades for charity or excellence in business. I'll take my trophy for a mayonnaise-based cheese recipe.

Now, the reason you may believe you hate pimento cheese is that your mother fed you the 1980s version from a tub in the grocery store, which was, categorically, a tragedy. I remember that gloppy mess. We should sue the food industry for ruining a perfect cheese food for an entire generation. Banish the memory if that's the only one you have, because this right here is your redemption.

// Shred your cheeses and drop them in a large bowl. Yay! Shredded cheese makes me so happy. If 16 ounces of freshly shredded cheese doesn't set your day right, just go to bed and start over tomorrow.

// Pile up the roasted red peppers and the jalapeños and chop them all together into little bitty pieces. (Sweet jalapeños are basically the bread-and-butter version of regular pickled jalapeños. Same idea, but canned with way more sugar, like our foremothers intended. They are really mild, so don't apply your precious spice sensibilities here.)

// Add the peppers to the bowl with the shredded cheese. Mix in ¼ cup each of mayo and yogurt, and if it's a little dry for you after mixing well, add some more of each. Some people like this creamier, some like it with less goop, so you get to be a grown-ass person who decides for herself. Stir in the mustard, pimentos, salt, pepper, and cayenne (if using).

// Let's talk about how to eat this. If it's for noshing, set this up with crackers, crostini, chips, a veggie tray, apple slices, charcuterie. If it's for zhuzhing, dollop it on baked potatoes, burgers, hot dogs, eggs, grits, rice, tacos, quesadillas, chili. If it's for a sandwich, please for the love, treat it like a grilled cheese, with crispy thick-cut bacon and homemade pickles grilled in butter to melty perfection. Or! Make your grilled cheese sammie with smoked ham and marmalade. Bless God. Bless him for making this food on his earth.

GREEN CHILE CHORIZO

Queso

One of the greatest days of my life was when my son Gavin got a job at Torchy's Tacos, where he worked for three years in college. Sure, he was busy getting a degree for a professional career, but he became an insider on Torchy's queso, which, by a margin of one thousand, is my favorite queso in the land. (Other children, take note: impressing your mother doesn't require anything more than working at her favorite restaurants. Turns out college is like, fifth place.)

In Kansas, where I grew up, "queso" meant Velveeta and a can of Ro-Tel. And that was the end of the tale. But then I moved to Texas in 1998, and I got converted and saved. Praise the Spirit for the Lone Star State when it comes to melted cheese snacks. Break out the tambourines!

This is a mash-up of the two best quesos in Austin: Torchy's and the Bob Armstrong dip at Matt's El Rancho. No additional commentary needed. If you know, you know.

Also, by the way, this makes a huge batch. These are party quantities, because I'm assuming you're making this for Football Saturday or Football Sunday or Football Monday. Cut it in half if you're planning to eat something other than cheese dip or feeding fewer than the million people who live in my house. But all leftover queso tells me is that I have something awesome to spoon over my eggs the next morning.

A word on chorizo: When readers ask me what chorizo is, I have to go into my prayer closet, because these poor souls are living in a state of deprivation. In short, chorizo is life. In long, chorizo is spiced ground pork, quite possibly the perfect food. Please do not buy the chorizo made from earlobes and assholes that's sold in a tube. It will ruin your day. If you can't get fresh ground chorizo or high-quality chorizo, just use ground hot Italian sausage.

1 pound ground chorizo (or ground hot Italian sausage)

2 tablespoons olive oil

1 small onion, diced

2 jalapeños, seeded and diced

4 garlic cloves, diced

—

1 (10-ounce) can diced tomatoes and green chiles (FINE, I USE RO-TEL), with their juices

2 (7-ounce) cans mild green chiles

1 bunch cilantro, chopped

1 (26-ounce) block processed cheese, cubed (FINE, I USE VELVEETA)

1 (12-ounce) can evaporated milk

1 cup half-and-half

2 tablespoons hot sauce

1 tablespoon ground cumin

1 tablespoon chili powder

Juice of 2 limes

1 to 2 cups water

// You can obviously tell just by looking at this ingredient list that you have stumbled upon the holy grail of queso. Of all the recipes in this book, I "tested" this one the most, mainly because I wanted to eat it the most.

// Brown the chorizo in a skillet over medium heat, 6 to 8 minutes, drain in a colander, and set aside (chorizo renders a lot of fat, and no one wants greasy queso). In the same skillet, combine your olive oil, onion, and jalapeños and sauté for 6 to 7 minutes, until the veggies start to brown. Add the garlic and sauté for 2 minutes more.

// I cook queso in my Crockpot like our ancestors intended, because it stays nice and warm and I can eat it for the next 6 hours. Combine the sautéed veggies and browned chorizo in your Crockpot, then add everything else on the list. How much water you add is up to you; it depends on however thick or not-quite-as-thick you want this queso to be. Cover the Crockpot and set it on High to speed up the melty process. As the cheese starts to melt, stir to combine. When you have it like you like it, turn your heat to Low and leave this on your counter aaaaaaaaaaall day.

// We like to drizzle a little Cholula on top because we play for keeps in Texas.

// I would serve this to Jesus if he came over for Football Saturday.

Honey Lemon Ricotta

with Toasted Hazelnuts

SWAP any toasted nut for the hazelnuts.

Not everything needs to be hard, dammit. Sometimes simple little appetizers are weirdly good, and that is the end of that. Plus, one time Ina Garten poured store-bought potato chips into a fancy silver bowl and served it to her guests (this memory is my inspiration and comfort, and I think about it fondly once a week). Using vintage or antique or quirky serving dishes for simple food is an absolute hospitality hack. Your guests will be like, "Oh! Look at this wacky little bronze serving bowl in the shape of a monkey head!" and they will forget to notice that you've filled it with shelf-stable vanilla wafers.

Speaking of Ina, I regret to inform you that I am about to employ the phrase "use the good ricotta, if you can." I'm sorry. I don't always call us to our higher consciousness, but occasionally, for the health and well-being of your dish, it's important to track down a superior ingredient. And let's be fair: I'm about to ask you to layer three plug-and-play ingredients in a bowl and put it on the buffet table, so let's not act like this recipe is labor-intensive. You have time to buy the good ricotta. (Check the cheese case at your grocery store or a little specialty shop.) (I'm also going to include instructions for making your own fresh ricotta and I don't want to hear about it.)

Zest and juice of 1 lemon

1 (15-ounce) container good-quality ricotta cheese

2 to 3 tablespoons honey, to taste

⅓ cup hazelnuts or pecans

Crackers or toasted baguette slices, for serving

// I mean, honestly. How is this a recipe. After zesting your lemon (set the zest aside), squeeze the fresh lemon juice into a bowl with your ricotta and mix. Spoon the lemon ricotta into your monkey head serving bowl. Drizzle the honey all over the ricotta. Toast your hazelnuts in a dry pan over medium heat for 4 to 5 minutes, coarsely chop, and let them cool, then scatter them over the honeyed ricotta. Sprinkle the lemon zest over the top. Serve with crackers or toasted baguette slices. I would actually eat this spooned over Cheerios.

Note

This is also a delicious spread for a tartine with sliced berries and chopped basil.

RECIPE CONTINUES

HOMEMADE RICOTTA

Yes, I am including instructions for this, because
it is dumb easy. Exhibit A:

**½ gallon whole milk
(don't fight me on this or
you will regret it)**

**⅓ cup fresh lemon juice
(from 2 large lemons)**

Pinch of salt

// Those are the ingredients. Here are the other very, very fancy things you need: a pot, a candy thermometer (which I don't even use but I am acting "formal" because cookbook editors say readers need "actual instructions"), and cheesecloth. Do you see what I'm saying? From start to finish, this takes half an hour and most of that is just waiting around.

// Warm your milk in a pot over medium heat until it reaches 200°F. If you're just eyeballing this, heat until it gets foamy and starts to steam, but don't let it boil. Take the pot off the heat, add the lemon juice and salt, and stir gently. Let it sit there for 10 minutes; it'll start to separate into chunky curds and watery yellowish whey. **And now you know why Little Miss Muffet sat on her tuffet. And now you also know that "curds" means "curdled." Don't be weird about it.**

// Line a strainer with cheesecloth and set it over a bowl. Slowly pour in the whole pot. Let the curds just sit there draining whey for anywhere from 10 to 30 minutes. You are in charge of this. If you want your ricotta a little looser, let it drain for a shorter amount of time. Want it firmer and dryer? Drain it longer. (If it gets too dry, you can add back some of the drained whey.) And that's it.

// If at all possible, let this cool a bit and then eat it right away. It's at its prime this minute. You can also spoon your ricotta into an airtight container and keep it in the fridge, where it will tighten up but still be delectable for up to a week. It is so scrumptious and fluffy and fresh and pure, you just won't believe it. PLUS, you get to tell your guests you made homemade ricotta, which you *know* they haven't ever done. You win.

Chicken and Beef Satay
with Peanut Sauce

A few years ago, my friends Jon and Laura threw a Thai dinner party, and it will go down as some of the best food of my life. Laura grew up in Thailand, so she was sure as hell not messing around with the recipes. Dinner was completely authentic and included about six courses, all of which were as hot as the surface of the sun. This is my entire love language: spicy Thai food in quantities that don't make sense for a normal person's consumption. This is how to love me. This is how to demonstrate loyalty.

Consequently, that was the first time I tasted peanut sauce, and it was like seeing the world in color for the first time. I mean, the color was brownish-tannish, so it wasn't that exciting to look at, but please just follow the metaphor. Plus, add marinated skewers of grilled meat? To dip?? This is how to live, man. This right here is your next happy appy, or put it over rice and call it dinner.

Note: Don't get weird about this ingredient list—most of it is dump and stir. The sauce is a no-cook whisk-and-serve. Once you have these ingredients on hand, they just live in your fridge and pantry, waiting to be turned into satay.

SATAY SKEWERS

1 (13.5-ounce) can full-fat coconut milk

5 garlic cloves, chopped

2 tablespoons chopped fresh ginger (you'll need another ½ tablespoon for the sauce . . . just saving you time here)

3 tablespoons brown sugar

1 tablespoon Thai yellow curry powder (not the same as Indian curry powder!)

1 tablespoon ground turmeric

2 tablespoons fish sauce

¼ cup soy sauce

Juice of 1 lime

Pinch of salt

—

1 pound boneless, skinless chicken thighs, cut into long, 1-inch-wide strips

1 pound beef skirt steak, cut *against the grain* into long, 1-inch wide strips

PEANUT SAUCE

½ cup creamy peanut butter

2 tablespoons soy sauce

Juice of 1 lime

2 to 3 tablespoons hot water

1 tablespoon brown sugar

1 tablespoon chili garlic sauce

½ tablespoon chopped fresh ginger

—

Chopped fresh cilantro, for serving (optional)

RECIPE CONTINUES

// Sure, both the satay marinade and the sauce have basically all the same ingredients. *It's called synergy, Susan.* Just put it all on your counter and make the marinade and the peanut sauce at once. Do this in the morning, or the night before, so literally all you have to do now is grill the meat for 10 minutes before serving.

// Start with the satay skewers—it's as simple as this: Throw all those ingredients ("coconut milk through pinch of salt") into your blender, blend on high, pour half over the sliced chicken in one container or large baggie and the other half over the beef in another, and stick them in the fridge. The end. Bye. See you later in my mouth. (But for real, you want the meat in this marinade all day or overnight.)

// Same for the peanut sauce: Combine it all and whisk. Buh-bye. But as always, this is to preference, so give it a little taste. You might want it sweeter (add brown sugar) or spicier (add chili garlic sauce). If it seems too thick, add another tablespoon of hot water until you like the consistency. If you make it early and it tightens up, just microwave it until it loosens back up. This sauce is so good, you guys. **I also drizzle this over leftover rice, use it as a raw veggie dip, spoon it over roasted veggies, and even use it as a salad dressing.**

// When you're ready to cook those skewers, heat your grill to medium-high. If you're using wooden skewers, soak them in water for 10 to 30 minutes while your grill is heating. Then take the chicken and beef out of the fridge and thread each slice of meat onto a skewer like you're sewing a hem. I don't know if this instruction makes sense because I don't sew, but do you know what I am saying? Like up, down, up, down. LOL. Bless me. Bless you. Bless this mess. Don't worry about it. Just thread them on there. And discard the marinade—it has done its work here. It has served you well, but we don't want salmonella, so fare thee well.

// Grill the skewers for about 4 minutes, until the meat is nice and grilled on the bottom, then turn and cook on the second side for 4 minutes (you may need less time on each side, depending on your grill). Oh, you won't believe how good it smells. Holy Moses.

// Get a large platter, plate up those beautiful skewers, and sprinkle with cilantro if you have it. Pour the peanut sauce into a cute serving bowl. I don't even care if my guests double dip—I will eat their secondary mouth mess with nary a concern, this is how committed I am to this particular food—but you can also set little plates out and they can serve their own. This is a slam-dunk winner. The world is in color!

Note

Add the Grilled Shrimp with Hot Honey and Coconut Rice (page 220) as the main dish, and this is a DINNER PARTY.

1 (12-ounce) package fresh
dates, pitted

1 (6-ounce) wedge
fresh blue cheese or log
of fresh goat cheese

12 ounces bacon (not
thick-cut)

8 ounces roasted almonds

Balsamic reduction (see
page 103), for serving
(optional)

BACON-WRAPPED DATES

STUFFED WITH BLUE CHEESE AND ALMONDS

I learned about these years ago from my dear friend Shauna Niequist, and I became an absolute pain in the ass until everyone I loved had tried them. I was insufferable and made them nonstop for six months. I mean, get serious: sweet dates, salty bacon, sharp blue cheese, and crunchy almonds? In one bite?? Like, literally get in my mouth.

These are the perfect nosh food because you can make them in advance and serve them at room temp. You don't need to add a damn thing to them, but I serve them with a little pitcher of balsamic reduction for drizzling or dunking in. **This is your next appetizer, and it is not up for debate.**

SWAP
cream cheese for
the blue cheese.

// Preheat your oven to 400°F and set a wire rack on a rimmed baking sheet. I bake these on a rack so the bacon fat drains. It makes for a nicer finished product with a little less grease, but if you don't have a rack, just lay those bad boys straight on your baking sheet. Are we really going to feel sad about bacon grease? We aren't.

// **This is an important instruction:** Pour a glass of your favorite wine and put on your favorite playlist, because you're going to stand in your kitchen making this little assembly line and you might as well enjoy yourself. Plus, you're making these for a party or guests or as your contribution to someone else's gathering, so it's time to get in the mood. You're welcome.

// With a paring knife, make a slit longways in each pitted date, without cutting all the way through. Dates were literally meant to be filled with cheese and nuts. Just look at that perfect pocket to stuff.

// **A quick word on the cheese:** Blue cheese is my soul mate and I will never get enough of it in all my earth years. I want it always and all the times. But some people have an aversion to moldy cheese for reasons I'll never comprehend, so if that's you, replace it with fresh goat cheese, because apparently you don't like mold but you're here for goat lactation.

// **A quick word on the bacon:** For every other bacon dish I can think of, I prefer Wright brand thick-cut bacon. It has no equal. But for this nosh, get the cheap thin stuff. We almost want the bacon to shrink-wrap the dates, and the thick stuff is too used to being the star. We want clingy, needy bacon with an inferiority complex. Cut your vulnerable bacon strips into thirds.

// With a spoon, put a little smear of blue cheese inside each date. Press a roasted almond right into the cheese. Close up the date and wrap a bacon strip tightly around the middle, then set it seam-side down on the rack. (You can skewer these with toothpicks if you'd like, but I find the bacon clings like a bad boyfriend.)

// Bake until the bacon is totally browned and the fat has rendered, anywhere between 15 and 25 minutes, depending on your oven.

// You can serve these warm right out of the oven, but good news! They're also delectable at room temp, so you can make them in advance, Party Queen. Drizzle with balsamic reduction and send me your thank-you cards. Oh, mama.

Coconut Shrimp

with Spicy Marmalade

This is the ten thousandth sweet-and-savory recipe I've included in this book, and I'm not nor will I ever be sorry, because coconut shrimp is incorruptible. I hope this will make up for the fact that my dessert chapter has exactly one entry. I may not have given you desserts, but I paired sweet things with jalapeños in approximately [[checks notes]] all the others, so that needs to count.

One time I ate so many coconut shrimp, I made myself sick. Like, a literal sick lady who had to lie down. I couldn't stop eating them, because the crunchy sweet succulent taste was too good. I'm just a person. Not a machine that can stop eating coconut shrimp just because there's no more room in her stomach. And here I am, still including them in this cookbook, because absolutely nothing can deter me from these, not even self-induced food poisoning.

Note

LEFTOVER SHRIMP?

Toast them back up in your toaster oven, slice, and layer over a salad the next day. Or toast them back up and tuck them into shrimp tacos the next night!

Nonstick cooking spray

—

1 cup orange marmalade

1 tablespoon prepared horseradish

1 tablespoon Dijon mustard

1 tablespoon hot water

Salt and black pepper

—

1 pound large shrimp, peeled and deveined

—

½ cup cornstarch

2 teaspoons cayenne pepper

3 egg whites, beaten with a mixer until foamy

2 cups sweetened coconut flakes

// We are going to bake these because we don't want the fried mess. The good news is, this coconut dredge crisps up beautifully in the oven, and the shrimp doesn't get overcooked. Plus, the fitness people will be like, *Yay! You baked instead of fried!* and we can be like, *Well, we also made chorizo queso and cheese pasta up in this piece, so just calm the eff down.*

// Preheat your oven to 375°F and spray a baking sheet with some nonstick spray.

// In a small bowl, whisk together the marmalade, horseradish, Dijon, hot water, and salt and black pepper to taste until smooth. Set aside.

// Rinse the shrimp and pat them dry, because that shrimp juice is kind of gross, let's be honest. Sprinkle the shrimp with salt and black pepper.

// In a shallow dish (I use a pie plate), mix the cornstarch, 1 teaspoon salt, and the cayenne. Pour the fluffy, beaten egg whites into a second shallow dish and dump the coconut flakes into a third (reserve some to add halfway through the dredging process so it doesn't clump too much). Assembly line: Dredge each shrimp in the cornstarch mix, then in the egg whites, then in the coconut flakes, making sure the shrimp is totally coated in each before moving on to the next. As you go, line up the dredged shrimp on your baking sheet so they're not touching.

// Bake for around 15 minutes or so, until the coconut is toasted, flipping the shrimp once at the halfway mark to make sure the coconut browns evenly. You don't want to overcook the shrimp, but if the coconut isn't brown enough for your liking after 15 minutes, turn on the broiler for a minute and toast them quick.

// Lay the shrimp on a lovely platter with the spicy marmalade in a little bowl for dipping. Disclaimer: You might accidentally eat so many that you have to put your undisciplined POS self to bed, but don't let this stop you, warrior. Believe in your dreams.

LINDSAY'S
CHICKEN WINGS
AND Blue Cheese

My sister Lindsay used to work in an office, until one day she hung up her cardigans and flew to New York for culinary school, because life is too short to pretend you care about Microsoft Excel when you don't. She did the whole thing and became a chef at a darling restaurant in Brooklyn where everybody knows your name.

The first time I went there, I was meeting my brand-new publicist Heather, who I had never met in person and wanted to impress. We had a big few days in New York for author stuff, and I suggested we meet at my sister's new restaurant, where we could be grown and important. No sooner did we sit down that Lindsay started sending out "pickle backs," which is a drink I know about now, because they will *put you under the table*. Dear Lord. I think I both cried and sang during that dinner, because that is apparently how I make a first impression.

Miraculously, Heather is still my publicist seven years later, and we are even, because during an ice storm on our next press trip to NYC, she put us in "our Uber," which turned out to be just some guy named Marty in a blue two-door Trans Am who pulled over for four fancy ladies standing in the cold. Three of us piled into the back seat, one in the front, and laughed until we cried. Thanks for not driving us to your sex dungeon, Marty.

Lindsay put these wings on her menu, and if I have eaten one, I've eaten forty thousand. These are so dialed in.

3 pounds chicken wings (I'm assuming you want a bunch)

3 tablespoons neutral oil

1 cup flour

1 tablespoon salt

2 teaspoons black pepper

2 teaspoons cayenne pepper (or kick it up if you like to party)

WING SAUCE

1 (17-ounce) bottle sriracha

½ cup maple syrup

1 stick butter, melted but slightly cooled (that is Lindsay's weird instruction)

BLUE CHEESE DRESSING

12 ounces blue cheese crumbles

1 cup mayo

1 cup sour cream

2 cups buttermilk (you might use less than the full amount; see Note on page 33)

1 teaspoon salt

Black pepper

// This feeds a crowd, because who makes wings for three people?

// Crank your oven to 425°F and let it preheat.

// Rinse your wings and pat them totally dry, then coat them with the oil. Put the flour, salt, black pepper, and cayenne in a large bag (I use an old-timey brown paper bag like I'm at the five-and-dime in 1957, but you can do this in a big bowl) and shake it up. Toss in your oiled wings. Shake shake shake. We just want these lightly coated.

RECIPE CONTINUES

// Grab a couple of baking sheets and a wire rack for each. Line the pans with foil and set a rack on top of the foil. (Your cleanup now equals trash-and-toss.) Pick up each wing with tongs, shake off any excess flour, and set on the racks in a single layer, not touching. Slide them into that hot oven and bake until the 20-minute mark, then flip and bake until they're crispy, brown, and sizzling, anywhere between 15 and 25 minutes more.

// While the wings are browning up, get your blender out for the two sauces.

1. **For the wing sauce,** combine the sriracha and maple syrup and blend. With the blender running, slowly drizzle in the melted butter. Take a quick taste. Want it sweeter? Add more syrup. (Not a sriracha fan? Use your favorite store-bought wing sauce. But you don't get to leave out the butter. Sorry. I don't make the rules.) Pour this into a large bowl and rinse the blender jar.

2. **For the blue cheese dressing,** combine all the blue cheese ingredients. Don't add the full pint of buttermilk right out of the gate—maybe start with half. Blend it up and see if you like the consistency of the dressing, then add more buttermilk to thin it if you prefer. Pour the dressing into a serving bowl.

// When your wings are done, put them in the bowl with the wing sauce and toss and toss to coat. Serve these with the bowl of blue cheese alongside for dipping. LORD, I would drink five pickle backs (again) and ride shotgun with Marty just to have these in front of me.

Note
PICKLE BACK

Fill one shot glass with 1½ ounces of Irish whiskey (like Jameson). Fill another shot glass with ½ ounce of pickle juice. Throw back the first, immediately followed by the second. And now you understand about the singing and crying.

Homemade Mozzarella Sticks

with Honey Mustard Dipping Sauce

Ask anyone who knows me what my trashiest, most indulgent, most juvenile guilty pleasure is, and they will tell you fried mozzarella sticks. This is a longtime obsession and, as it turns out, an irreversible one. The WAY I love these things. I used to buy a Costco-size box of them, stick them in the back of the freezer, and eat every.single.one. Crunchy, oozy, stringy, gooey. The best best best.

And riddle me this: If I grabbed a string cheese stick from the fridge, the kind we throw in our kids' lunches, I would eat one. I would peel off its little tendrils and nibble on it for 5 minutes. But if those refrigerated cheese sticks get breaded and fried? I will eat twelve if I eat a single bite. **In your living life, can you imagine eating even six string cheeses? Well, you're about to, so gird your loins.**

If you put these out as an appetizer, they will be gone instantly. These are the facts.

1 cup flour

1 tablespoon salt

—

2 eggs, beaten

3 tablespoons milk

—

1 cup panko bread crumbs

1 teaspoon dried basil

1 teaspoon dried oregano

1 teaspoon dried parsley

1 teaspoon garlic powder

—

1 (24-count) bag mozzarella string cheese

Vegetable or grapeseed oil, for frying

HONEY MUSTARD DIPPING SAUCE

¼ cup honey

¼ cup mustard

¼ cup mayo

1 tablespoon white vinegar

Dash or two of cayenne pepper

Pinch of salt

Could also serve with marinara or ranch for dipping.

RECIPE CONTINUES

// This is a simple dredge-and-fry, but there is a trick or two you're required to obey. First of all, the breaded mozzarella sticks will need to go into the freezer for at least an hour before frying, so build that time in. Otherwise, they'll melt out of their breading jackets and your day will be RUINED.

// **Set up three shallow dishes (I use pie plates) for your dredging station:** the flour and salt in one; the eggs and milk, beaten to combine, in the second; and the panko, basil, oregano, parsley, and garlic powder in the third. Coat each cheese stick with the flour, then dip in the egg mixture, then coat in the panko, then back into the eggs, then back into the panko. Really press it all on. Tip: Use one hand for the dry dredge and the other hand for the wet dredge to keep your hands from becoming a breaded freaking mess. Also, dredging gets clumpy, so keep extra ingredients on hand to add more if your stations start to act a fool. You can always add another beaten egg or more panko to the mix. Whatever gets your cheese breaded, man.

// **Trick 1:** Every millimeter of the cheese (ends included) needs to be covered with the dredge, or that cheese will ooze out of the breading.

// **Trick 2:** The double dredge. This is like dressing your cheese sticks in two jackets so they won't freak out in the oil.

// **Trick 3:** After you double dredge each cheese stick, lay them on a baking sheet in a single layer and stick them in the freezer for at least an hour. This way, the cheese just melts in the hot oil instead of turning to liquid cheese that wants out of its jacket.

// **Make the dipping sauce:** Whisk together the honey, mustard, mayo, vinegar, cayenne, and salt in a small bowl until smooth and delish. Set aside until ready to serve.

// Preheat your oven to 200°F. Fill a Dutch oven or other large pot with about 2 inches of oil and heat the oil to 325°F.

// Working in batches, fry your mozzarella sticks until toasty brown on all sides, 2 to 3 minutes total, turning them over halfway through. Transfer to a paper towel–lined baking sheet and keep warm in the oven until you're through with ALL 24. Don't you dare buy the 12-count bag.

// Serve these hot, obviously. It is the cook's prerogative to eat the first eight before calling the troops. You work hard. You deserve this. You are a real winner. Plus, dairy is good for your bones. This is for your health.

3

FOOD *FOR* SPOONS

SAUCES & SOUPS

FRENCH ONION SOUP

A few years ago, I flew to Chicago for a weeklong culinary boot camp at the Chopping Block, where ten of us cooked for forty hours and drank around 283 bottles of wine. From my cozy hotel room a block away, I wrote about my exploits online every night, and one of my readers said it was like reading letters from summer camp. Thus, I dubbed it Food Camp, and so it remains, because an important part of being a writer is stealing ideas from other people.

Because we're on the subject, here are the three main lessons I learned that week:

1. Turn up the heat way higher than you think you should.

2. Stop stirring so much.

3. Add more salt and fat.

I had no idea how severe my stirring addiction was, but Food Camp taught me to let the thing sit on the heat and brown, for gosh sake. **"Stop stirring the pot" is apparently a real thing and not just what the internet ladies tell me when I get riled up.**

Which brings me to this particular page. I'm trying to think about what other recipe in this cookbook I am more thrilled you are about to make, and I'm struggling to find one. There is not a single reason you should not make French onion soup tonight. It is the most delicious, delightful soup of all the soups. This is not a matter of opinion, but fact. Come at me. Also, it's the easiest thing. This recipe (more or less) came from Food Camp, and I have never been happier to hand $1,200 to anyone in my life.

4 tablespoons (½ stick) butter

5 large yellow onions, sliced

Salt and pepper

—

3 garlic cloves, chopped

3 tablespoons flour

⅔ cup sherry or dry red wine

6 cups beef stock

2 tablespoons chopped fresh thyme

—

Loaf of French bread, sliced thick

3 to 4 cups shredded Gruyère cheese (12 to 16 ounces)

> ***Note*** This is 100% best on day 2, so it's a perfect make-ahead soup.

RECIPE CONTINUES

// Heat a big soup pot or Dutch oven over medium-low heat. Drop in the butter and let it melt, then add the onions and season with salt and pepper. (A word: This will seem like a preposterous amount of onions. "No one wants this many onions in anything," you will say. That is a lie. Please be patient with the volume of onions. If you skimp on the onions, you will regret it for the rest of your life.) Cook these down until they are brown, caramelized, beautiful things. Like 45 minutes. (Chef Lisa at Food Camp said she doesn't have time for this nonsense, and she cranks the heat to high and blasts her onions into submission. Please live your life accordingly.)

// Stir in the garlic and cook for 1 minute. Sprinkle in the flour and stir for another minute. Pour in the sherry to deglaze the pot, then scrape, scrape, scrape. YOU DON'T WORK FOR YOUR ONIONS, THEY WORK FOR YOU.

// Pour in the stock. At Food Camp, we made our own. Ina Garten INSISTS that we make our own, or how are we any different from the animals? I am here to tell you that I make almost everything from scratch, and *I use grocery store stock* because my freezer is too full of garbage Hot Pockets and frozen waffles, and I am now rethinking my previous "everything from scratch" declaration.

// Raise the heat to high (if it isn't there already) and bring the stock to a boil, then lower the heat and simmer for 15 minutes. Add the thyme and season with 1 tablespoon salt and pepper to taste.

// This is when it gets exciting.

// Preheat your broiler and cover a baking sheet with foil. Set individual ramekins on top (6 or 8 of them, however many you're serving) and ladle the soup into the ramekins. F.O.S. is literally why ramekins were invented.

// Place thick slices of French bread on top of the soup in each ramekin until it covers the whole top. Load an irrational amount of shredded Gruyère onto the bread. This is more exciting than new Royal babies. (Some people put the bread in the ramekin first, pour the soup over, then top with the cheese. But which is best: delicious surprise bread at the bottom, or toasty cheesy bread on top?? My response to this dilemma is this: What a wonderful time to be alive when this is the biggest problem of your day. This is not a legitimate bone of contention.)

// Carefully slide the baking sheet onto the middle rack of your oven and broil. Watch the tops carefully: when the cheese is a melty, gooey avalanche, it is dinnertime.

// Everyone gets their own ramekin, which makes them feel special and fancy. Pair French onion soup with a bright, crunchy salad, and you are now such a culinary hero that even Ina will forgive you for the boxed stock.

Habanero Cream Soup IN A BREAD BOWL

Once upon a time, my marriage fell apart and my girlfriends booked and paid for a trip to Mexico, where they gave me a homemade shirt with a Photoshopped picture of me and Jason Bateman ironed onto it, because I had once told them he was my perfect male archetype. (It included a swoopy heart graphic that said "I love you more," which they explained to me as "you love Jason more because he has never heard of you.")

While at MB Restaurant at our resort, Live Aqua, upon good intel from the internet, we ordered the habanero cream soup and promptly lost our minds. It was served in a homemade bread bowl and topped with fried potato chips, and when I tell you we LICKED our plates . . . I left not a drop of soup but actually left half my bread bowl uneaten, and Megan deadpanned to my face: "I've lost all respect for you."

The very living day we got home, I scoured the World Wide Web for the restaurant's exact recipe to put immediately into my Test Kitchen. I found a very dubious handwritten gem "loosely" translated from Spanish with such quantities as "seven habaneros" and "three cups of flour," but reader, any recipe with seven habaneros would put your family in the ER. So I tweaked and altered and prioritized our stomach linings, and I did it. I give you habanero cream soup so perfect I would serve it to Jason Bateman.

2 habanero chiles

2 jalapeños

2 poblano peppers

1 onion, quartered

4 garlic cloves, peeled

⅓ cup olive oil

Salt and black pepper

—

1 cup (2 sticks) butter

1 cup flour

4 cups chicken stock

4 cups whole milk

1 to 2 cups water (depending on how thick you want your soup)

1 teaspoon freshly grated or ground nutmeg

—

8 ounces spinach (maybe 4 big handfuls)

—

Juice of 1 lemon, plus more if needed

—

8 bolillos or small sourdough loaves, or any hearty bread that can be hollowed out for individual bread bowls

—

1 cup heavy cream

// Preheat your oven to 400°F.

// Wearing gloves (habanero juice on your fingers when you rub your eyes later will ruin your day), halve and seed your habaneros, jalapeños, and poblanos. Throw them onto a baking sheet with the onion and garlic, drizzle with the olive oil, and sprinkle with salt and black pepper. Roast for 20 to 25 minutes. This will mellow out the heat and sharpness of these flavors and make everything jammy and caramelly and yummy. (Leave the oven on if you'll be making bread bowls.)

// In the meantime, in your Dutch oven, melt the butter over medium heat, then whisk in the flour until incorporated, around 2 minutes. Add the stock, milk, water, nutmeg, 1 tablespoon salt, and pepper to taste (I want to taste buckets of pepper) and whisk until smooth. Lower the heat and cook, stirring, until the mixture starts to thicken up, around 5 minutes.

RECIPE CONTINUES

// Dump in the roasted peppers, onion, and garlic. Add the spinach and cook until it is wilted, around 2 minutes. Remove from the heat.

// Working in batches, pour this deliciousness into your blender and blend until super smooth (with no visible green spinach bits, which is why I don't love the immersion blender for this one). Yes, this means you'll need to pour the first batch of pureed soup into another container until the rest is pureed, which is a pain in the ass, but the reason we had children is so they would do the dishes.

// Pour the pureed soup back into the pot, set it over low heat, and add the lemon juice. Give it a quick taste and see if you'd like a bit more salt. If it tastes at all flat, see what adding a bit more lemon and 1 teaspoon salt does. Acid and salt are Food CPR.

// If you're absolutely going for it, hollow out individual loaves of bread (don't break through the bottom) and cut whatever bread you scrape out into cubes. Throw the bread bowls and their cubed innards on a baking sheet and toss them into the oven for 5 minutes, until toasty.

// Fill each bread bowl with soup and drizzle with heavy cream. Put the "innard croutons" on the side for maximum dipping and carb loading. This soup is so beautiful, you will want to make an iron-on shirt with its picture.

// Or just pour it into a bowl and shove it in your face hole.

// May the universe bless you with girlfriends who take you to Mexico when your heart is shattered and feed you pepper and cream soup and dress you in absurd manifestations to walk you all the way to new life.

Note

Want to spice down? Use Hatch chiles or poblano peppers in place of the jalapeños.

CORN AND Leek Bisque

6 ears fresh, delicious summer corn

4 tablespoons (½ stick) butter

2 cups sliced leeks (white and light green parts only; discard the root and stalky ends), rinsed well to remove any grit

—

1 jalapeño, minced

3 garlic cloves, chopped

4 cups chicken stock or veggie stock

2 bay leaves

1 teaspoon cayenne pepper

Salt and black pepper

—

2 cups heavy cream

FOR GARNISH

1 cup snow peas, thinly sliced crosswise

1 cup chopped fresh tomatoes

Heavy cream, for drizzling

1 cup chopped fresh cilantro

When people say they don't want soup in the summer because it is too hot, I am curious if they only eat cold food for three months. Do they eat room-temperature hamburgers? Does pizza need to be cold? Can we no longer grill our steaks? Why does everything else get to be hot in July except soup? Everyone needs to back off this injustice and dial it back right now, because this summer soup is downright dreamy. **You will eat this soup piping hot in your flip-flops and you will like it, dammit.**

Is this an okay time to say I don't like cold soup at all? Don't @ me with gazpacho. I said what I said. It is so unsatisfying. Whoever invented cold soup is just mean. That is a mean person. This is why we can't have nice things. No, I don't want to eat your cold cucumber soup, either. Yuck. Why. If I'm eating something cold out of a bowl, it better damn well be ice cream, or you're going to stick that gazpacho in the microwave.

Note Pair this with a bright summer chopped salad with a lemon vinaigrette.

// If you're making this in January, you're allowed to use frozen sweet corn (one 40-ounce bag, thawed), but if you live within 50 square miles of fresh summer corn, you will cut kernels off those cobs or die trying. Fresh corn is literally the point of this recipe. Just hold the cob vertically on your cutting board and slice a sharp knife down the sides. Yes, the kernels will go everywhere and this takes more time than opening a bag from the freezer, but we make these kinds of sacrifices because we are incredible people. (Ina once suggested standing the cob upright in a bowl to catch the naughty, wayward kernels you cut off, but I'm always trying to do the least number of dishes, so I just collect my kernels from the four corners of the earth after slicing them off.)

// Melt the butter in a skillet over medium heat. Add the leeks and sauté until they are tender, around 8 minutes. Set aside ½ cup of the corn kernels for serving and add the rest to the pan with the leeks, along with the jalapeño and garlic. Cook for 2 minutes, then add the stock, bay leaves, cayenne, 1 teaspoon salt, and black pepper to taste. Raise the heat and bring this to a boil, then lower the heat, cover, and simmer for 20 minutes to let the flavors meld.

// Remove the bay leaves. If you want this soup super smooth and creamy, transfer it to a blender in batches and puree. If you want it a little more rustic (I refuse to say "chunky" when discussing a liquid food), just use an immersion blender.

// Back in the pot, add the cream to the soup and warm it through on low.

// Ladle the soup into bowls and pile up the reserved corn, crunchy snow pea strips, and tomatoes on top. Drizzle with cream, sprinkle with cilantro, and serve. The right word for this soup is *darling*. I swear if you don't absolutely love this dish in the dead middle of summer, I will eat gazpacho every day for the rest of my life.

BUTTERNUT SQUASH Ginger Carrot Soup

My grandparents gardened, so I grew up on a steady diet of yellow squash and zucchini. My grandma layered them in a casserole with butter and covered them in Ritz crackers, of course, so I thought all squash was medium to low in flavor and easily cooked into mush. I didn't experience butternut squash until I was grown. I also didn't know pumpkins were a squash, as this is not readily apparent, I don't care what you say. I've since become familiar with the concepts of "summer squash" and "winter squash" because I am a person able to learn things, but my real point here is that butternut squash is the best of them all.

I put butternut squash into the highest rotation. It adds the exact sweet and tender je ne sais quoi I always want in my savory food, and it is an absolute dream in soup. You are going to make this soup in the fall while wearing a cable-knit sweater in a cozy mountain cabin with a fire in the fireplace and a good old dog at your feet. I am manifesting this for you.

Note

I love butternut squash, but I will tell you it is a bitch to cut up. You can do it, of course, because with God, all things are possible, but guess what? Our grocery stores sell cubed butternut squash in containers, and this is a hack I subscribe to.

1 large butternut squash, peeled and cubed (6 to 8 cups)

4 carrots, sliced

1 large onion, coarsely chopped

4 tablespoons olive oil, plus more for drizzling

Salt and pepper

—

5 garlic cloves, chopped

2 tablespoons finely chopped fresh ginger

1 tablespoon dried thyme

4 cups chicken stock or veggie stock

1 (13.5-ounce) can full-fat coconut milk

—

2 to 3 cups cubed bread (any bread you have: sandwich bread, leftover rolls, buns, something going stale . . .)

Heavy cream or sour cream, for serving (optional)

Pomegranate seeds, for garnish (optional)

// What takes this soup over the top is roasting the veggies first, so preheat your oven to 400°F.

// On a rimmed baking sheet, toss the butternut squash, carrots, and onion with 3 tablespoons of the olive oil and sprinkle with salt and pepper. Roast those gorgeous root vegetables for anywhere around 30 minutes, until the squash and carrots are fork-tender. This deepens their flavors and develops the sugars. Remove from the oven (keep the oven on).

// After the veggies are roasted, in a Dutch oven or other large pot, heat the remaining 1 tablespoon olive oil over medium heat. Add the garlic, ginger, and thyme and sauté for around 3 minutes, until fragrant but not browned. Add the roasted veggies and any yummy flavored oil left on the pan. Stir to combine, then add the stock, coconut milk, 1 tablespoon salt, and pepper to taste. Bring to a boil, then lower the heat, cover, and simmer for 15 minutes to let the flavors meld.

// I like this soup with a little bit of texture, so grab your immersion blender and zip this up. If you prefer it entirely smooth, you can do this in batches in your blender. Give it a little taste and adjust the seasoning if you need to.

// On a rimmed baking sheet, toss the bread cubes with a drizzle of olive oil and a sprinkle of salt. Toast them up in your already-hot oven for a few minutes until browned and crunchy.

// Serve this soup in cozy bowls with a pile of homemade croutons, topped with a drizzle of cream (or dollop of sour cream if you'd like it a little tangier) and a scattering of pomegranate seeds, if desired. Crack fresh pepper over the top, too. I don't know what a "cozy bowl" is, but I'm assuming it is in your mountain cabin. Eat this dreamily under a fuzzy blanket while watching the season's first snowfall from your picture window.

OLD FASHIONED
Beans and Cornbread

My parents didn't have a lot of money when I was a kid, but I had no idea. The way they scraped and scrapped and scrimped was well outside my purview. I loved childhood and lived in the "fun house." Sure, I never got the *one pair of Guess jeans* I begged for, since Mom said she would book a one-way ticket to Communist Russia before spending $50 on a pair of pants for a ninth grader (Russia played prominently in the '80s childhood experience), but it never dawned on me that my parents budgeted so carefully.

As a mom to five kids, I now understand that feeding a large family costs roughly equivalent to the entire GDP of the USSR. I mean, dear Lord in heaven. So many mouths. So much hunger. Such enormous portions. So many mouths. Hindsight explains my mom's penchant for serving a giant pot of beans and a cast-iron skillet of homemade cornbread. The entire operation costs around $7, soup to nuts, but the end result is SO SATISFYING. To this day, I loooove a pot of beans and will dunk a butter-soaked piece of cornbread into it with such delight it almost heals me from my Guess jeans trauma.

One pair, Mom.
I made straight A's.
I got saved at church camp every single summer.
I deserved them.

2 (16-ounce) bags dried pinto beans

Salt

—

1 onion, chopped

3 carrots, chopped

3 celery stalks, chopped

5 or 6 garlic cloves, coarsely chopped

1 hunk of a cured ham hock (or any smoked meat chunk or bone)

2 chicken bouillon cubes

2 tablespoons brown sugar

⅓ cup chopped fresh herbs (thyme, rosemary, sage, oregano, whatever you have, in any combination)

1 bay leaf

A Parmesan rind, if you have one (otherwise, now you know—save your next one)

CORNBREAD

1 cup fine or medium-grind yellow cornmeal

1 cup flour

1 tablespoon granulated sugar

1 teaspoon salt

3½ teaspoons baking powder

1 egg, beaten

1 cup milk

⅓ cup butter (about 5 tablespoons), melted, plus more for the pan

FOR SERVING (OPTIONAL)

Olive oil, for drizzling

Pickled or fresh jalapeños

Sour cream

Chopped white onion

Hot sauce

RECIPE CONTINUES

// Beans can be cooked in a Crockpot, in an Instant Pot, in the oven, or on the stovetop, and they'll turn out delicious. **I repeat: all beans are good beans.** By way of personal preference, I like beans to hold their shape a bit, so this is my fave method. It means you're going to soak your beans overnight and not act like that is a hardship. Can you pour water into a bowl? Your work here is done.

// So: The night before, rinse your dried beans, pick out any obvious stinkers, pour them into a pot, add water to cover them by 3 to 4 inches, and throw in a big handful of salt. That's that. Let them go to bed in their delicious salt bath.

// About 2 hours before you want to serve your beautiful beans, drain and rinse them, transfer to a Dutch oven or other large pot, and add fresh water to cover by about 3 inches. Add the rest ("onion through Parmesan rind"). Bring to a boil, then lower the heat, cover, and simmer for anywhere between 2 and 3 hours, until the beans are tender but still hold a bit of shape.

// **Cornbread time:** This is just like making pancakes. I love baking this in my cast-iron skillet, but you can use a 9-inch round cake pan. Preheat your oven to 400°F and go bananas buttering your cast iron (or cake pan).

// Whisk together the cornmeal, flour, granulated sugar, salt, and baking powder in a large bowl. Make a well in the center and add the egg, milk, and melted butter to the well. Whisk until smooth. Pour the batter into your buttered pan. Bake for 20 to 25 minutes, until a knife stuck into the center comes out clean.

// Right before serving, remove the bay leaf and ham hock from the beans, cut the meat off the bone and shred it up, then add the meat to the beans.

// This is humble, simple food that doesn't need to be improved upon. It is scrumptious and nourishing and chock-full of flavor. Now, if you added a spoonful of chow-chow (see page 105), I wouldn't be mad (chow-chow and beans are BFFs), but one bowl of these gorgeous beans, drizzled with olive oil and married to a hunk of buttered cornbread, is everything that is right with the world. The only righter thing would have been a damn pair of Guess jeans in 1988.

Leftover beans? LUCKY. Here are some ideas:

- ✦ Use as a base for taco bowls.
- ✦ Turn into burritos.
- ✦ Layer on a crostini with sliced red chiles, a sharp cheese, and a drizzle of olive oil.
- ✦ Sub for the black beans in the Sweet Potato and Black Bean Burgers on page 169.
- ✦ Turn them into gratin with toasted bread crumbs.

Tom Kha Gai

SWAP
1 tablespoon lemongrass paste for the fresh lemongrass.

What is the best food in the world, and why is it Thai food? If I made a random list of all my favorite individual ingredients and combined them to see what happens, I would end up with tom kha. You guys, the first time I ever ate this soup, I stood straight up at the table like I was moved by the Holy Spirit in church. *I had no idea.*

If it isn't clear yet, sweet-and-savory-and-spicy is my favorite flavor profile, which is so weird, because I don't really like dessert. I only want sweet if it's in bed with sliced jalapeños or spicy mustard. One time I was in Haiti with my compatriots, and one of our meals ended with a bowl of chocolate ice cream. Casually, nonchalantly, like she wasn't about to change my life, my friend Kristen reached over and sprinkled kosher salt over her ice cream. I tried it on one bite, and reader, I tell you, I AWOKE AND LIVED. This was ten years ago and I *still* ramble to Kristen about it, and she still pretends to care.

Here we go, soup makers. Game time.

Never bought lemongrass or fish sauce or red curry paste? Don't worry about it. Your grocery store has it all, and now you're supporting the lemongrass industry, which wants more home cooks to make tom kha.

1 tablespoon coconut oil or other high-temp oil

1 onion, sliced

3 garlic cloves, thickly sliced

1 red or green jalapeño, or 2 fresh Thai chiles, thickly sliced

1 (2-inch) piece fresh ginger, thickly sliced

1 lemongrass stalk, whacked with the blunt side of your knife on all sides (called bruising) and cut into 2-inch-long pieces

1 to 2 tablespoons red curry paste, to taste

4 cups chicken stock

4 cups coconut milk (full-fat, of course, we aren't fools; it's a little less than three 13.5-ounce cans)

2 boneless, skinless chicken breasts, thinly sliced

8 ounces sliced mushrooms

2 tablespoons sugar (I like coconut sugar for this, but who has that?)

2 tablespoons fish sauce

Juice of 2 limes

Salt and pepper

FOR GARNISH

Sliced scallions

Sliced red jalapeños or fresh Thai chiles

Chopped fresh cilantro

RECIPE CONTINUES

// Melt the coconut oil in your Dutch oven over medium-high heat, then throw the onion, garlic, jalapeño, ginger, lemongrass, and curry paste into the coconut oil. Your knife cuts here can be a nightmare and everything can be large chopped, because you're just flavoring the broth. You're going to strain all this out, so who cares if it's uniform? I don't even peel my ginger. Cook, stirring frequently, for around 5 minutes, until the veggies are softening up.

// Add the stock, bring it just to a boil, then reduce the heat, cover, and simmer for 30 minutes. All those delicious aromatics are turning that boxed stock into the soup base of your dreams. This flavored broth is the magic of tom kha.

// Strain the broth to remove the solids, then return the broth to the pot (or scoop out all that stuff with a large slotted spoon). Add the coconut milk to the broth and bring it up to heat. Add the chicken and mushrooms and poach for about 4 minutes, until the chicken is no longer pink. Finally, add the sugar, fish sauce, and lime juice and season with salt and pepper. Taste this and see if you want to add anything. It should be creamy, tangy, spicy, and slightly sweet.

// Ladle this majestic soup into individual bowls and top with scallions, chiles, and cilantro. This is restaurant-quality food. This is dinner party food. This will make your people stand straight up at the table and declare you their queen.

Notes

Add bright, crunchy spring rolls with peanut sauce from the Chicken and Beef Satay with Peanut Sauce recipe (page 65) for dipping, and this is a meal fit for the gods.

DRESSINGS

It was an absolutely shocking moment when I learned mortal people could make their own dressings. I literally had no idea. I thought ranch was made at Hidden Valley in their secret labs and our only portal was the grocery store. Turns out, homemade dressings are super easy, pretty formulaic, and taste around 100% better. You almost always have everything you need to make them. They also don't have ingredients like "natamycin" or a tiny aftertaste of plastic. From now on, you will be a homemade dressing person. This is who you are now.

My fancy tool for dressings is a mason jar with a lid. When I have an herby dressing, I use a blender. This marks the end of your kitchen appliance tutorial.

For each of these dressings, put all the stuff in your mason jar and shake or into your blender and puree. This marks the end of your homemade dressing tutorial.

One last thing: All dressings are to taste and preference. You can make them thinner or thicker or spicier or tangier; you can add more garlic or less, more sugar or none. I've written these the way I like them, but you can absolutely adjust them however you want. **Number One Rule of Dressing Club: There is a Dressing Club and you are now a member and all members taste and adjust.** Your dressing, your house, your choice. No one tells you how to live.

SPICY RANCH

Makes 1½ cups

Ranch is so American. Maybe we should be embarrassed that we dip even our pizza into this dressing, but whatever, haters. This is America! We'll ask for ranch for our steaks in a fine-dining establishment if we want to! This recipe is for spicy ranch, which is a bit kickier, but just leave out the cayenne and boom: regular ranch, like the pilgrims ate.

1 garlic clove, peeled

1 teaspoon kosher salt

1 teaspoon freshly cracked black pepper

1 teaspoon dried dill

1 teaspoon dried onion flakes

½ teaspoon cayenne pepper

½ cup sour cream

½ cup mayo

⅓ cup buttermilk (see Note, page 33)

⅓ cup fresh parsley (no need to chop or stem it)

1 tablespoon fresh lemon juice

2 shakes of Worcestershire sauce

2 or 3 shakes of hot sauce (all hail Cholula)

Throw everything into the blender, blend, and get ready to live. If you dial back the buttermilk, this will be thicker and you can use it as a dip. Or add more buttermilk if you want a thinner dressing.

CREAMY BLUE CHEESE

Makes 1 cup

If you don't love blue cheese, we're in a fight. My thruple husband, Tray (see Tray's Tomato Pie, page 160), makes his salads into what he calls "blue cheese soup," where the lettuce is literally swimming in blue cheese dressing. This is both gross and awe-inspiring.

3 ounces blue cheese

3 tablespoons buttermilk (see Note, page 33)

⅓ cup mayo

⅓ cup sour cream

1 tablespoon white vinegar

1 teaspoon sugar

¼ teaspoon garlic powder

Salt and pepper

Put the blue cheese in your mason jar and mash slightly with a fork to break it up. Add the rest of the ingredients, pop the lid on, and shake and shake and shake. Stir a bit before pouring, as the blue cheese settles on the bottom. This is the absolute prom queen of wedge salads and chicken wings.

HONEY MUSTARD

Makes ¾ cup

Honey mustard is my favorite food. This is my flavor profile. I will put it on virtually anything. It is my dip, dressing, and sauce of choice. You can make this as mustard- or honey-forward as you want. I love to load up a salad with creamy, salty, and savory stuff and let the sharp honey mustard win the day.

2 tablespoons Dijon mustard

2 tablespoons honey

¼ cup extra-virgin olive oil

Juice of ½ lemon

Salt and pepper

Everything goes into your mason jar. Shake it like a Polaroid picture until it's all incorporated. Give it a taste and see what you think. You can mellow it out with a bit more olive oil or a touch more honey, but I like this to slap me in the face. Building your salad, think: avocados, roasted pecans, goat cheese, crumbed bacon, and sliced hard-boiled eggs. Add grilled chicken or shrimp, and this is dinner, jokers.

GREEN GODDESS

Makes 2 cups

I originally tried this after watching Ina make roasted shrimp with Green Goddess dip on her show, and for the first time in my life, I bought anchovy paste. This is a path of growth. Don't panic. **If you can buy tomato paste, you can buy anchovy paste, and now you know the world is full of possibility.**

Also, this dressing is thick and gloppy (a technical term). It stands up beautifully to super-hearty lettuce but overpowers the sensitive, fragile stuff. I actually love this most as a dip alongside a whole platter of crunchy veggies, or as Ina calls them, *crudités*. People who buy anchovy paste serve crudités. Into the blender:

1 cup fresh parsley (no need to chop or stem it)

1 cup watercress or spinach

2 tablespoons stemmed fresh tarragon leaves

3 tablespoons chopped fresh chives

1 garlic clove, peeled

1 teaspoon anchovy paste, or 2 anchovy fillets

3 tablespoons fresh lemon juice

1½ tablespoons champagne vinegar or white wine vinegar

½ cup olive oil

½ cup mayo

Salt and pepper

Zip this up in your blender until smooth, and just look at it. Isn't she lovely? The dressing will keep for 3 days in a jar in the fridge.

CAESAR DRESSING

Makes 1 cup

SPEAKING OF ANCHOVY PASTE, look at you, now in possession of two recipes requiring your brand-new tube of salty deliciousness. Once you make this Caesar, you'll start living a whole new life. Don't overreact to the whisking steps here. If whisking is the hardest thing you do today, that's a pretty damn good Tuesday.

¼ teaspoon coarse salt

2 garlic cloves, peeled

3 egg yolks

1 teaspoon Dijon mustard

2 teaspoons anchovy paste

2 tablespoons fresh lemon juice

2 tablespoons extra-virgin olive oil

½ cup grapeseed oil

3 tablespoons finely grated Parmesan cheese

1 teaspoon pepper (Caesar looooves black pepper)

Sprinkle the salt over the garlic cloves on your cutting board and, with the flat side of a knife, press the garlic into a smooth paste. Set this aside.

In a medium bowl, whisk the egg yolks until smooth and glossy, about 2 minutes. Whisk in the mustard. Whisk in the garlic paste. Whisk in the anchovy paste. Whisk in the lemon juice.

While whisking continuously, slowly drizzle in the olive oil until it is incorporated and emulsified. Repeat this slow whisking process with the grapeseed oil, then keep whisking for another minute until the dressing is perfectly thick.

Stir in the Parmesan and pepper, and try to forgive me for using the word "whisk" 10 times in 135 words. This is a whole reason to put chicken Caesar salad on your menu this week.

CHAMPAGNE/BALSAMIC/APPLE CIDER VINAIGRETTE

Makes ¾ cup

People, listen: vinaigrettes are almost identical, and you change up the flavor by changing up the vinegar. It is that simple. Subtle and floral? Champagne vinegar. Rich and sweet? Balsamic vinegar. Sharp and tart? Apple cider vinegar. I could keep playing this game, but I believe in your capacity to think through what vinegar tastes like and use it in your vinaigrette.

You could liven up any vinaigrette with fresh herbs (finely chopped) or a tablespoon of minced shallot, and all the flavors can be dialed up or down depending on your preference. I love vinegar-forward dressings, but some folks prefer a ratio of 1 part vinegar to 2 parts oil. Dressings are FLEXIBLE. As long as you combine oil and vinegar, everything else in your mason jar is a flavor bonus.

1 garlic clove, minced

2 tablespoons Dijon mustard

2 tablespoons honey

¼ cup whatever your vinegar is

¼ cup extra-virgin olive oil

Juice of ½ lemon

Salt and pepper

You know the drill: Combine all the ingredients in a jar, cover, shake.

PLUM AND BLUE CHEESE SALAD WITH WARM BACON VINAIGRETTE

Serves 4 (makes ¾ cup vinaigrette)

I saved this dressing, and the salad that goes with it, for last because it is speeeeeecial and probably one you haven't tried. In a world of cold salad dressings, this warm vinaigrette is elevated and different and interesting. This makes the most gorgeous brunch salad next to a wedge of frittata and a grapefruit mimosa. I would make out with you if you served me this for brunch.

———

1 (5-ounce) bag baby spinach (this wilts a bit with the dressing)

2 plums, pitted and sliced into thin wedges

¼ cup slivered almonds, toasted

2 ounces crumbled blue cheese (¼ cup)

———

3 thick-cut bacon slices

2 tablespoons olive oil

1 shallot, minced

2 tablespoons red wine vinegar

1 tablespoon whole-grain mustard

½ teaspoon brown sugar

1 teaspoon chopped fresh thyme

Salt and pepper

———

8 slices prosciutto, cut into wide strips

This salad is best served while the dressing is warm, so have the rest of it assembled before you start the bacon: In a wide, shallow serving bowl, arrange the spinach and plum slices, then scatter with the almonds and blue cheese. (Plums out of season? Crisp apple slices are a delicious substitute.)

Cook the bacon in the olive oil in a skillet over medium heat until crispy, then transfer to a paper towel to drain, leaving all the fat in the pan. Still over medium heat, add the shallot, vinegar, mustard, brown sugar, thyme, and some salt and pepper and whisk until smooth. Remove from the heat and let the dressing cool for 2 minutes.

Crumble the cooked bacon over the salad, gently toss with the warm dressing, and arrange the sliced prosciutto in folded pieces over the top. THE MOST GORGEOUS.

Note

The vinaigrette is also delicious drizzled over Brussels sprouts, green beans, roasted potatoes, or grilled radicchio quarters.

SAUCES AND RELISHES

In general, I believe most food is simply a vehicle for sauce. One of the proudest moments of my life as a young mom was watching my kids put ketchup on their cheeseburgers, then squirt a pile of "side ketchup" for additional cheeseburger dipping. I mean, I don't know if they'll contribute to society or have happy lives, but they will never eat dry food, and that counts for something. Hell, in addition to this short section, I have fifteen other recipes that include sauces in this cookbook. Big fan of dipping, drizzling, dunking, and smothering.

Here are a few multipurpose sauces and relishes you can use in a million ways.

BALSAMIC REDUCTION

Makes ¾ cup

It's a real stretch to include this in a cookbook, but I just can't explain how delicious balsamic reduction is on virtually everything. It's like a rich, sweet syrup that I literally have in my fridge at all times. It is very, very hard to make (sarcasm).

1 (16-ounce) bottle decent balsamic vinegar   **1 tablespoon sugar**

In a small saucepan, cook the vinegar and sugar over medium heat until reduced by about two-thirds. It will be bubbling. No need to stir. One whole bottle will only make a little baby pitcher of reduction. If there is any trick to this, just know that balsamic reduction can go from syrupy perfection to gummy in record time. At the 10-minute mark, start checking it. You'll know it's ready when it coats your spoon and has the consistency of syrup. It should also taste mostly sweet, not mostly acidic, but PSA: let it cool on your spoon longer than 3 seconds before your taste test. Why can't I learn this. Why.

This will keep in an airtight container in your fridge for a couple of weeks, but it won't last that long. Here is a nonexhaustive list of things to drizzle with your balsamic reduction: pizza, eggs, any of the tartines in this book (see page 118), ricotta, avocados, roasted potatoes, sweet potatoes, butternut squash, green beans, Brussels sprouts, literally any salad, any of the mayo-based sammies in this book (see page 110), creamy soup, ice cream, strawberries, pork chops, grilled chicken. I would drizzle this over plain buttered toast, and by "would," I mean "have."

TRASH SAUCE

Makes ½ cup

Well, hell, we named it this because it is. (My daughter Remy is a much sweeter member of our family, and she calls it "special sauce.") This has no right to be delicious, yet here we are. This is a poor man's rémoulade and absolutely does in a pinch.

¼ cup mayo   **2 tablespoons ketchup**

1 tablespoon Dijon mustard   **Pinch each of salt and pepper**

Put everything in a bowl and whisk!

You'll see I've elevated this sauce elsewhere in this book in such delightful recipes as Homemade Corn Dogs and Trash Sauce with Relish (page 138) and Diner Cheeseburger Sliders with Hot Trash Sauce (page 155) because I am fancy. You can tweak this by adding sriracha, or sweet chili sauce, or fresh lime juice, or hot sauce, or horseradish. This is our tip-top favorite condiment for cheeseburgers and fries. I love it with fried shrimp, boiled crawfish, chicken sandwiches, roasted veggies, hash browns, onion rings, veggie burgers, fried fish, all the things.

HOUSE SAUCE

Makes 6 cups

Okay, that's it. We're not effing around with Trash Sauce anymore (page 103). You know I hate to be dramatic (lol), but this tomato/marinara sauce is all my dreams come true. I make this once a week. **I'll include the doubled recipe quantities, because if you aren't doubling your House Sauce to freeze half for next time, you need to go to church and get saved.**

First, a word about the tomatoes: I use Muir Glen, and there is nothing you can say to change my mind. Just do not get some janky tomatoes from the bottom shelf. I am so serious. In the summer, fresh, homegrown tomatoes would be the star of this recipe, obvs, but are we really going to boil and peel twenty tomatoes when we can just open a can? We are not.

½ cup extra-virgin olive oil

1 teaspoon red pepper flakes

6 large or 8 small garlic cloves (not at all sorry), chopped

—

1 (28-ounce) can organic tomato puree

1 (15-ounce) can organic crushed tomatoes

2 to 3 tablespoons balsamic vinegar, to taste

1 to 2 tablespoons sugar, to taste (start with 1 tablespoon)

Salt and pepper

—

2 tablespoons cornstarch (optional)

Combine the olive oil, red pepper flakes, and garlic in a Dutch oven or other large pot over low heat and cook for 3 minutes, until it starts to smell like heaven's kitchen. Add the tomato puree, crushed tomatoes, vinegar, sugar, and salt and pepper to taste and whisk, whisk, whisk until all that delicious flavored oil is incorporated. This takes longer than I like, but we have to incorporate the oil entirely so it doesn't separate.

Turn the heat up and bring the sauce to a boil, then drop it back down to low, cover, and simmer for 1 hour. The flavors develop after cooking, so let it be for a while, then taste, taste, taste. All those measurements are up for grabs, by the way. You get this sauce how you like it; taste and adjust the sugar, vinegar, and spice to YOUR LIKING.

This is my go-to red sauce for all things pasta/Italian, but if you want your sauce a little thicker for pizza, more like a marinara (which I do), make a quick slurry by whisking 2 tablespoons cornstarch into a bit of water, then stir it into the sauce at the end. It will thicken up the whole pot like magic.

Remove from the heat and let cool, then pop half the sauce into a zip-top bag or airtight container and freeze it for next time. (Hell, make a VAT of this and store 8 portioned containers in the freezer. Future you will thank vat-of-House-Sauce you.)

CHOW-CHOW

Makes about 8 cups

I recently found out that chow-chow is Southern. I thought everyone knew about the most delicious relish in the whole of the world. Oh man, you guys. Grilled summer hot dogs cherish the day chow-chow walked into their lives. It is tangy, sweet, spicy, and crunchy—in other words, the perfect relish. Don't get flustered by the length of this ingredient list. Most of it is in your spice cabinet already. Plus, I just gave you three-ingredient Trash Sauce (page 103), so you can make room in your heart for chow-chow.

Y'all, chow-chow is positively delicious on hot dogs and bratwurst, or spooned over grilled pork chops, chicken, or fish. It livens up a bowl of beans like your favorite party friend who shows up with margaritas. Dollop it on burgers, pulled pork sandwiches, or shrimp tacos. Your omelet will *preen* with a scoop of chow-chow. Spoon a cup or two over a block of softened cream cheese and serve it with buttery crackers. Just YUM.

5 cups white vinegar	**1 teaspoon ground turmeric**
3 cups sugar	
2 tablespoons kosher salt	**1 teaspoon red pepper flakes**
1 tablespoon ground cloves	**1 bay leaf**
	—
1 tablespoon mustard seeds	**4 green tomatoes, diced**
1 tablespoon black peppercorns, crushed	**2 green bell peppers, diced**
1 teaspoon mustard powder	**1 red bell pepper, diced**
	1 sweet onion, diced
	½ head green cabbage, diced

In a large pot, combine the vinegar, sugar, salt, cloves, mustard seeds, black pepper, mustard powder, turmeric, red pepper flakes, and bay leaf and bring to a boil, then reduce the heat and simmer for about 5 minutes, until the sugar has completely dissolved.

You want your veggies all diced roughly the same size, a pretty fine dice. It looks like a huge pile of veg, which it is, but it'll cook down quite a bit. Add the veggies to the pot, bring back to a boil, then lower the heat and simmer for 15 minutes, stirring occasionally. Remove the bay leaf and divide your chow-chow and its liquid among a few jars (or other lidded containers), however big or small you want them to be (these would be the cutest little party favors in miniature jars). Seal and refrigerate. Chow-chow keeps easily for a week in the fridge.

TEXADELPHIA MUSTARD BLEND, I GUESS

Makes ½ cup

Perhaps no other entry in this cookbook took as much R&D as this one.

When I moved to Austin in 2000, the very first restaurant I ate at was Texadelphia, a local gem specializing in cheesesteaks. I have eaten roughly four tons of their signature item: The Founder's Favorite with Mustard Blend, a soft, melty, spicy concoction of seared beef, mushrooms, jalapeños, and sautéed onions on a soft grilled roll.

But the Mustard Blend, y'all. The living best. AND APPARENTLY TOP SECRET.

Lord, the sleuthing I did to find this recipe. I was so deep on message boards and Reddit and secret threads, I think I became part of the deep state. Not ONE former Texadelphia employee was willing to spill the exact details on the internet somewhere? Not *one*? No, good reader, they were not. So I gathered whatever sketchy intel was out there and put it into test-kitchen mode. I can't explain why this is as delicious as it is, since the ingredients are bizarre, but dear Lord.

¼ cup mayo	**2 teaspoons teriyaki sauce**
3 tablespoons spicy brown mustard (I like Gulden's)	**1 teaspoon honey**

Whisk all this together, and that is the end of the Texadelphia Mustard Blend saga. As always, you can adjust to your preference, but drizzle this over a Philly cheesesteak and get ready to become an evangelist. This will keep in your fridge nicely for a week.

4

FOOD *THAT* GOES IN CARBS

SANDWICHES, SUBS & TACOS

French Dip Subs

The first time I ever ordered a French dip sandwich at a restaurant, I asked the server what "awe juss" was (maybe fancy mushrooms, or a complimentary side of V8?). Turns out, it was just delicious beef juice, and I was a real Basic Becky. I grew up in Haysville, Kansas, okay?

I've since put French dip sammies into high rotation up in this piece, because they are nearly the perfect sandwich. They turn out badly never, they're absolutely awesome for feeding a crowd, they make your house smell magical, and they improve your mood on game day even if your team loses (see: Texas Longhorns) (see: Kansas City Chiefs).

Salt and black pepper

4 pounds chuck roast

1 (1.5-ounce) packet pot roast seasoning (whatever, haters)

—

2 large onions, sliced

¼ cup olive oil

1 (16-ounce) jar sweet cherry peppers, drained and sliced

GARLIC-SCALLION MAYO

1 cup mayo

2 garlic cloves, minced

2 tablespoons chopped scallion

Salt and black pepper

OR

LEMON-HORSERADISH MAYO

1 cup mayo

1 tablespoon prepared horseradish

Juice of 1 lemon

Salt and black pepper

—

8 sub rolls

24 ounces sliced cheese (my faves, in order: provolone, Swiss, pepper Jack, cheddar—use what you like), 3 or 4 slices per sub

// I like to start my roast first thing in the morning, because it is impossible to cook it too long. Salt and pepper your chuck roast. Get out your handy-dandy Crockpot, drop in the chuck roast, and just dump that packet of seasoning right in, then add water to come 2 inches up the side. (Listen, do not get elitist with me about the seasoning packet. Last time I checked, I am a grown woman who can do what she wants.) Cover the Crockpot, set it to Low, and cook that roast all damn day (but not less than 5 hours), which is exactly how it wants to be treated.

// About an hour before dinner, get those onions caramelized. Caramelized onions are my life partner. Sweet and brown and jammy and perfect. I would eat a plate of them for dinner. In a big skillet, sauté the onions in the olive oil over medium-low heat for 45 minutes. Add the cherry peppers toward the end and cook until warmed through.

// Just before dinner, transfer the roast to a big baking sheet and shred it with two forks. Cook's note: I am fanatical about discarding every tiny bit of fat during this process. If I bite into a chunk of fat inside my sandwich, you tell 'em I'm comin' and HELL IS COMIN' WITH ME (I pledge allegiance to *Tombstone*). My sister did shred duty the last time I made these, and she said fat is an important part of the flavor, but she's just a chef so what does she know.

// Pick your awesome mayo: garlic-scallion mayo or lemon-horseradish mayo (they're exactly what they sound like). Dump those ingredients into your mayo, stir, season with S&P, and now your fancy mayo is complete.

// Get some yummy sub rolls from your bakery and slice them lengthwise almost all the way through. **Load up your rolls like this:**

1. Your fancy mayo.
2. Slices of cheese, 2 of them to start. This acts as a juice barrier so your bread doesn't get too soggy from the beef. Brené Brown taught me that boundaries are important.
3. Shredded beef, devoid of any trace of fat. You're welcome.
4. Caramelized onions and peppers. Dear Lord.
5. More sliced cheese. Because 'Merica.

// Load the sammies onto a baking sheet and stick them under the broiler for a couple of minutes, until the cheese is all melty and the bread gets crusty.

// This makes every human person happy. If you want to get real serious, strain the cooking liquid you left behind in the Crockpot and give the people ramekins of au jus. Or you can be trashy like my family and just dip your sandwich straight into the Crockpot, because if you offer an au jus ramekin to someone from Haysville, they will punch you in your fancy face.

MAYO-BASED-"SALAD" SANDWICHES

Leave it to the South to engineer a mayonnaise-based spread and call it a "salad." Tra-la-la! We'll do what we want! I, for one, am entirely here for it. At almost all times, I have one of these "salads" in a container in my fridge, because I eat sandwiches every single day for lunch, and these are my favorite.

There are several crossover ingredients, but the most important thing to know is that you need good mayonnaise. *Here* is where I should probably include a how-to on making your own mayo from scratch, because it *is* actually easy, but *here* is where I tell you that I love Duke's brand and I don't want to make my own mayo and I don't think you want to make your own mayo, and the moral of this story is that I buy Duke's and will forevermore. Can't *something* be processed??

CHICKEN SALAD ON CROISSANTS

Serves 6

1 whole rotisserie chicken

—

1 cup mayo

2 tablespoons Dijon mustard

2 to 3 tablespoons white vinegar, to taste

1 to 2 tablespoons sugar, to taste

1 tablespoon poppy seeds

Salt and pepper

—

1 cup chopped celery (2 or 3 stalks)

½ cup sliced scallions

½ cup slivered almonds, toasted

½ cup dried cranberries, or 1 cup grapes, halved

FOR ASSEMBLY

6 croissants

Butter lettuce leaves

Tomato slices

You bet your ass I use store-bought rotisserie for this. Chicken salad is the reason rotisserie chicken was invented. If you can, pull the chicken meat from the bones while it is still warm from the bosom of your grocery store, because it falls right off. Discard all the skin and bones, and either shred the meat or cut it into bite-size chunks. (I'm not trying to tell you what to do, but shred it. Shredded chicken is so pleasing!) You should end up with 4 to 5 cups.

In a large bowl, whisk together the mayo, Dijon, vinegar, sugar, poppy seeds, and salt and pepper. This dressing is totally to taste, so taste it and see, chicken salad maker! You can make this sweeter or tangier or creamier or saucier. Your kitchen, your rules.

Add the chicken, celery, scallions, almonds, and cranberries and stir gently until well combined. Dear LORD, the way I love this. Super love it on a croissant with butter lettuce and ripe tomato slices doused with salt and pepper. I also love the first four spoonfuls I eat right out of the container because I am "taste testing."

TUNA MELTS ON SOURDOUGH

Serves 6

The '70s called and they want us to make tuna melts again. You don't get to protest this recipe if you haven't had this sandwich in twenty years. There's a good chance these used to be weird when we were kids, but it is a new day, campers. I late-night ordered a tuna melt at some random little diner in Manhattan a couple of years ago (I think there had been some . . . wine?), and I have been unable to cure my obsession since. Crispy, melty, creamy, crunchy . . . these are a dark horse crowd-pleaser.

3 (5-ounce) cans tuna packed in olive oil, drained

¼ cup mayo

1 tablespoon Dijon mustard

2 celery stalks, finely chopped

¼ cup finely diced red onion

2 tablespoons dill pickle relish

3 to 4 tablespoons chopped fresh parsley

Salt and pepper

—

2 slices sourdough bread per person

2 slices cheddar cheese per person

Sliced ripe tomatoes

Softened butter, for grilling

Is three cans of tuna too many? I don't know how to make small amounts of food. Don't worry about it, because the only thing better than a tuna melt is another one the next day. **Also, hot-take alert: I _deeply_ prefer tuna packed in olive oil over tuna packed in water.** It adds tons more flavor. Canned tuna in water makes me have sad feelings.

In a medium bowl, combine the tuna, mayo, Dijon, celery, onion, relish, parsley, and some salt and pepper. Taste and decide if you want to adjust anything. I don't like it too goopy because then it slides out of my sandwich even though I try to glue it in with double cheese.

I reeeeeeally like sourdough for this sammie. You can obviously use any bread you like, but grilled sourdough holds up perfectly and delivers the most satisfying buttery crunch in the whole Western Hemisphere.

Build your melts like this: bread, cheddar slice, tuna mix, tomato slices (which you will obviously salt and pepper, because you aren't a maniac), one more cheddar slice, bread. Melt tons of butter in a skillet or on a griddle over medium heat and drop in your sandwiches. Grill until toasty and melty on each side, around 4 minutes per side. You simply _must_ cut your sandwich in half on the diagonal just to look at this beauty. The sound of biting into a crunchy tuna melt is my new ringtone.

EGG SALAD ON TOAST

Serves 6

This is the second time I've written about egg salad in a book, because the very second I think the thought "egg salad," I have to have it within the hour. It is an incurable disorder. I am never going to get through writing this recipe, dammit.

Now, listen: you will need way more eggs than you think. There's some sort of egg sorcery that means when you fry an egg, you eat one or two like a normal human person. But when you turn them into deviled eggs (or their squashed-up version: egg salad)? You eat no fewer than seventeen, possibly more. Easily. You won't even be full. I don't understand this because I make a living with words, but it is poultry science. When someone volunteers to bring deviled eggs to one of our family gatherings, we're like, "Make around six times more than you think you should, or don't bother coming."

12 eggs

½ cup mayo

1 tablespoon Dijon mustard

⅓ cup sweet relish

⅓ cup chopped sweet pickled jalapeños (also called bread-and-butter jalapeños)

Tons of salt and pepper

Buttered toast, for serving

To make foolproof hard-boiled eggs: Put your eggs in a saucepan and add cold water to submerge them by about 2 inches. Bring to a full roiling boil, then turn off the heat, cover, and leave the eggs in the hot water for 10 minutes. Drain the hot water and run cold water over the eggs right in the saucepan to cool them. Then it's peeling time.

Drop your peeled eggs into a large bowl and mash them willy-nilly with the back of a fork. Very recently, my friend Jenny acted SHOOK when she learned I mash my eggs. She claimed that eggs get chopped into uniform pieces for egg salad. She said this like it was Egg Salad Law and I had committed a crime. Well, I am here to tell you I like my eggs smashy, and my name is on the front of this book, so smashy it is.

Add everything else (use more or less of any of it) and stir gently until totally combined. That's it. Eat this for every meal until it's gone. My favorite way to eat egg salad is on buttered toast, and I shall not be moved. But also on crackers, in a tortilla wrap, over lettuce or spinach, with celery sticks (some people like this, but it sounds devastating), or straight out of the bowl with a spoon, because 4 eggs equals none in egg salad.

Pulled Pork Sliders

with Spicy Slaw

1 cup barbecue sauce (any kind you love)

½ cup apple cider vinegar

½ cup chicken stock

¼ cup packed brown sugar

1 tablespoon Worcestershire sauce

1 tablespoon Dijon mustard

1 tablespoon chili powder

1 tablespoon ground cumin

2 teaspoons dried thyme

1 large onion, coarsely chopped

4 garlic cloves, chopped

1 (3- to 4-pound) boneless pork shoulder

Salt and pepper

SPICY SLAW

½ cup mayo

2 tablespoons spicy brown mustard

2 tablespoons apple cider vinegar

1 to 2 tablespoons sugar, to taste (start with 1 tablespoon, then taste and adjust)

½ teaspoon ground cumin

A few dashes of cayenne pepper

Salt and black pepper

—

1 (14-ounce) bag coleslaw mix (I like green and purple cabbage with carrots)

2 jalapeños, halved lengthwise, seeded, and sliced into half-moons

2 scallions, thinly sliced

FOR SERVING

Hawaiian buns or slider rolls

Piiiiiiiiiiiickle slices (my son Caleb and I say bread-and-butter pickles are indispensable)

I am absolutely fanatical about pulled pork. Fuh-na-ti-kull. I love it with vinegary Kansas City barbecue. I love it with sweet Texas barbecue. I love it with mustardy Carolina barbecue. I love it with creamy mayonnaise slaw. I love it with pickled Asian slaw. I love it with cider vinegar slaw. I love pulled pork on bread, in sliders, in tortillas, on buns. For me, the combo of rich-saucy-tender with crunchy-tangy-spicy is undefeatable. Pulled pork: 100. Haters: 0.

To be clear: I think pulled pork sliders should be a sloppy hot mess. The meat juice should be a disaster on your plate, the slaw drizzling everywhere, pickles coming out every which way, a mess. You do not eat these on a first date. You eat them hunched over a picnic table in your uncle Ronnie's backyard while your kids sneak the last sips of everyone's beer. This is Trashy Fam Food, and I live for it.

This feels like a long list of ingredients, but it's just stuff you have. It comes together in your Crockpot in 5 minutes. Also, I'll give you quantities because [[checks contract]] I have to, but this is actually imprecise. Just squeeze and dump and shake and throw it all in there. Who cares?

// This feels like a lot but it isn't. You're going to chop exactly four things and everything else is a dump. I even gave you a bagged coleslaw mix.

// Guys, I can't quit my Crockpot. I know the modern kids use their Instant Pots, and I get it. I do. But I am still in love with my off-white ceramic Crockpot from 1997. It is low-tech and outdated, exactly like my paper calendar and my AOL email address. I don't care. This is who I am.

// **Here is your morning work:** From the ingredient list, dump "barbecue sauce through chopped garlic" into your Crockpot and whisk to combine. Rinse the pork shoulder, pat it dry, and salt and pepper it, then nestle it in the Crockpot. Roll it around a time or two to get that sauce all over. Put the lid on, set the heat to High, and let this cook for 5 to 6 hours, until the pork shreds easily with a fork.

RECIPE CONTINUES

// **About an hour before dinner, make the slaw:**
In a bowl, whisk together the "mayo through salt and pepper" until smooth. Add the coleslaw mix, jalapeños, and scallions and toss until totally combined. So. For less money and more food, you could buy and shred your own cabbage and carrots. But sometimes life is hard and we need something to be easy. Thank you for listening. Stick the spicy slaw in the fridge to let the flavors come together. I love it best at the 1-hour mark.

// Your pork is now falling apart. It is perfection. Throw it on a baking sheet and shred the meat with two forks. *As mentioned* I don't like fat and weird things in my shredded meat, so I discard any of that ish. Then right back into the juice all that shredded meat goes. Put your Crockpot on Warm to keep this dinner ready.

// Preheat your oven to 350°F.

// Slice your buns and toast them cut-side up in the oven for a few minutes, until they're just starting to turn toasty brown. You can skip this, of course, but a toasted bun really stands up to this sloppy deliciousness.

// **Buffet time:** slider bun, juicy tender pork, giant pile of saucy spicy slaw, pickles. This is everything you want it to be. Uncle Ronnie better get his paper plates and PBR ready, because it is on.

> # Note
>
> Leftover pulled pork should absolutely go into a frittata the next morning. It could clearly also turn into carnitas, which is reason alone to make too much.

TARTINES

God, I love Austin. It is the weirdest little corner of Texas
that isn't little at all anymore since every single one of you
moved here in the past ten years. You're all here now. I see
you. The secret of Austin is out, and now it's home to the entire
world population and we're all driving on I-35 every day, which
is the single reason I have lost my salvation.

Digressing.

This city has been my homeland for over two decades, and it
is my favorite place on earth. It's an eater's heaven. So many
chefs have set up camp here and opened restaurants and food
trucks and pop-ups. Including French bistro Blue Dahlia, one of
our local gems, which is the first place I ever saw "tartines"
on a menu. I obviously first ordered their egg salad with capers
tartine (see: my egg salad disorder, page 113), but I've since
eaten all nine tartines on their menu because I finish the shit
I start. Tartines are fancy French open-faced sandwiches with
ingredients artfully arranged on hearty bread (for Pinterest, I
assume), and they deserve a place in our culinary hearts. Here
are three of my absolute faves.

ROASTED FIG AND RICOTTA TARTINE WITH LEMON, THYME, AND HONEY

Makes 4 to 6

2 tablespoons honey

Juice of 1 lemon (zest it first!)

1 tablespoon olive oil

Pinch of salt

8 ounces fresh figs, cut into slices that will lay flat on a piece of bread

—

1 small loaf rustic bread (French or sourdough), sliced pretty thick

1 cup ricotta cheese

½ cup hazelnuts (or pecans or almonds or cashews), toasted and chopped

Zest of 1 lemon (remember how I told you?)

1 tablespoon chopped fresh thyme

Flaky salt

Author Danielle Walker (buy her cookbooks immediately) and I were having lunch at Kim Paisley's house one time, and Danielle put halved grapes for our salad on a baking sheet and stuck them in the oven. **Roasted fruit? Is a thing?? It is.** I will forever credit Danielle for showing me this magic trick.

Preheat your oven to 400°F.

In a small bowl, whisk together the honey, lemon juice, olive oil, and salt. Toss the sliced figs in this goodness, put them in a single layer on a baking sheet, and roast them for 7 to 8 minutes. Remove from the oven. Now you have roasted figs. Roasted figs are a thing.

Increase your oven temp to broil. Lay your bread slices in a single layer directly on your oven rack. Just toast those gorgeous slices until lightly browned. Stay vigilant, home cook! Don't walk away! This only takes between 1 and 2 minutes.

Spread your dreamy ricotta over each slice. You will obviously be heavy-handed with this, because the only thing better than ricotta is more ricotta. Spoon the roasted figs over the ricotta, then sprinkle with the hazelnuts, lemon zest, thyme, and flaky salt. And why wouldn't you drizzle it with a little more honey? Please, I beg you, take this tartine's picture like it's posing at Olan Mills like our moms made us do in the '80s.

> *Note* Can't find fresh figs? You can use pitted dates. Or rehydrate dried figs and use those. Google will tell you how!

ROASTED VEGETABLE AND HUMMUS TARTINE

Makes 4 to 6

1 red onion, thinly sliced

1 yellow bell pepper, thinly sliced

1 red bell pepper, thinly sliced

1 cup sliced asparagus (cut on an angle into 2-inch-long pieces)

3 tablespoons olive oil

3 tablespoons balsamic vinegar

Salt and pepper

—

1 small loaf rustic bread (French or sourdough or multigrain), sliced pretty thick

1 container traditional hummus (or make your own! I gave you a killer recipe on page 54)

1 container crumbled feta cheese

1 bunch parsley, chopped

Preheat your oven to 400°F.

Toss all your sliced veggies on a baking sheet with the olive oil, vinegar, and salt and black pepper to taste. Roast for 25 to 30 minutes, until your veggies are caramelized and just as tender as you like them. Remove from the oven.

Crank the oven temp to broil. Lay your bread slices right on the oven rack to toast for 1 to 2 minutes, until browned and crunchy.

Spread each slice with a hearty dose of hummus, top with a generous pile of roasted veggies, and sprinkle with some feta and parsley. Look at her. What a beauty. What a star.

MUSHROOM AND GRUYÈRE TARTINE

Makes 4 to 6

3 tablespoons butter

3 tablespoons flour

1 cup milk

1 tablespoon Dijon mustard

Pinch of freshly grated nutmeg

Salt and pepper

—

3 (8-ounce) packages mushrooms (get 3 different kinds! Life is wild!)

3 tablespoons olive oil

3 tablespoons butter

2 tablespoons chopped fresh thyme

1 bunch parsley, chopped

—

1 small loaf hearty bread (I like sourdough for this one), sliced pretty thick

—

4 ounces Gruyère cheese, shredded (1 cup)

In a large skillet, melt the butter over medium heat. Whisk in the flour and stir for a minute. While whisking, slowly add the milk, then whisk until it is incorporated and smooth. Add the Dijon, nutmeg, and salt and pepper to taste. Cook, whisking, for another 3 minutes or so, until the sauce thickens up. You want this down-and-dirty béchamel kind of tight because it'll be the base layer for this tartine. Pour it into a bowl and set aside.

Slice and dice your mushrooms so they're all a similar size. Let's wipe out that same skillet and use it again. Toss in the butter and olive oil and heat over medium heat to melt the butter, then throw all those yummy mushrooms into the pool along with the thyme and parsley. Stir until the mushrooms are coated with the butter and oil, then let them sit on that heat to brown and render their moisture. All I can hear is Chef Lisa from Food Camp (see page 81) in my ear: "STOP STIRRING SO MUCH. LET THE DAMN FOOD COOK." You want the mushrooms browned and shrunken like little old ladies in Florida.

Set your oven to broil. Lay your thick slices of bread directly on the oven rack in a single layer to toast for a couple of minutes. Remove them from the oven and line them up on a baking sheet. Spread about a tablespoon of the béchamel on each slice, load them—and I mean LOAD them—with your delicious mushrooms, and absolutely pile a mountain of Gruyère onto each.

Slide your tartines back under the broiler. Watch them closely, because you know how precarious broiling can be. When the cheese is a melty avalanche and starting to brown and bubble, they're ready for ravenous consumption. Add a leafy salad and this is dinner, ladies and gents.

GARLIC BUTTER Italian Sausage Subs

These are so over-the-top fantastical. I already told you unironically that sandwiches are my favorite food, and this right here is why. This Italian sub is soft and melty and rich and saucy and toasty. It is gorgeous to look at. It smells divine. You know instantly you are about to be a delighted eater. I want these on football days with giant piles of salty chips and freezing ice-cold Shiner beer. Voilà! Perfect game-day food.

Fun fact: When my eldest son was in college, he texted me the following: "Do I have what I need to make rice?" (Bless.) I texted back, "All you really need is rice, twice that amount of liquid, and voilà!" **He replied, "I don't have any voilà. I don't even know what that is."** Jesus, take the wheel.

Reader, look at the separate words in the title of this recipe: Garlic. Butter. Italian. Sausage. Subs. These should comprise the five levels of the new food pyramid. Remember how the bottom level used to be "grains" and we were instructed to eat at least eight servings a day? Nutritionists were like, "Greens? Half an ounce. Processed bread? A loaf a day." This probably explains my sandwich obsession. I was brainwashed by the Wonder Bread lobby.

SAUSAGE MIXTURE

2 tablespoons olive oil

1 small onion, chopped

1 pound ground hot Italian sausage

3 garlic cloves, chopped

1 teaspoon red pepper flakes

1 cup dry red wine

3 cups House Sauce (page 104; this needs an hour, so start it early or make it in advance)

Salt and black pepper

1½ cups chopped fresh basil (reserve ½ cup for garnish)

GARLIC BUTTER

1 cup (2 sticks) butter, at room temperature

2 tablespoons chopped fresh basil

1 large garlic clove, chopped

FOR ASSEMBLING THE SAMMIES

6 soft sub rolls, sliced lengthwise but not all the way through (like a hot dog bun)

12 slices provolone

12 slices mozzarella

½ cup chopped red onion

RECIPE CONTINUES

// **Make the sausage mixture:** Heat the olive oil in a skillet over medium-high heat, then add the onion and sausage and sauté until the sausage is browned, 6 to 8 minutes. Add the garlic and red pepper flakes and stir for 1 minute. Add the wine and cook to reduce it, about 2 minutes. Finally, pour in the House Sauce and season with a generous dose of salt and black pepper. Turn the heat to low and let this simmer for 15 minutes. Turn the heat off and stir in 1 cup of the basil (reserve the rest for garnishing the sammies). **This saucy, meaty mixture can now become a million things. Pour it over noodles, layer it between lasagna noodles, sauce your English muffin pizzas, fill your zucchini boats or stuffed peppers, make an Italian shepherd's pie, smother your baked potatoes, use for Shakshuka (page 50), the sky's the limit.**

You can dial the sauciness up or down with more or less House Sauce.

// Meanwhile, preheat the broiler and combine your garlic butter ingredients in a bowl.

// To assemble your sammies, slather the inside of each sub roll with a ton of garlic butter and load them onto a baking sheet, sliced-side up. Slide the pan onto the lowest oven rack and broil for about 1 minute, until the butter has melted.

// Take the rolls out of the oven and layer each like this: 2 slices of provolone, sausage mixture, 2 slices of mozzarella. Pop the subs back under the broiler for about 3 minutes, until the cheese has totally melted and is starting to bubble and the rolls are toasty on top. Don't walk away from these, home cook. The broil stage of any recipe is precarious. It's like, "Getting there, getting there, perfect, BURNT!"

// Sprinkle the subs with the onion and reserved basil. Grab your favorite crunchy chips, pop the top on an ice-cold beer, and voilà!

Life has no real meaning if you aren't making and eating po'boys. This is my favorite recipe. And let me say up front: battering, breading, and frying food is such an ordeal, an *ordeal*, I say, so I only do it when the taffy is worth the pull, and trust me, it's worth it here. This will make a real mess, and you will still write me and say "THANK YOU, JEN HATMAKER." One final note: Don't you dare look at this ingredient list and turn the page because it feels too long. Almost all of this is in your spice rack and the door of your refrigerator. Everyone calm down.

This feeds eight. Halve it if you're feeding fewer people than I am, which is probably everyone. Dear Lord.

SPICY CAJUN SHRIMP Po'Boys

We moved to Houma, Louisiana, the summer before my fourth-grade year, and on the second night we were there, we went to a crawfish boil and ate alligator. It was the most extra thing that had ever happened to me in my whole life of nine years. Having hailed from a region where the adjective "spicy" was added to a menu item if it had any black pepper in it, this was completely off the rails. I'd never even seen a bottle of hot sauce. We were real culinary cream puffs.

Anyhow, it took about one week to discover po'boys, and we bought our first batch literally from a shack next to the bayou (I fact-checked this with my dad, and the credibility is "dubious," but honestly? Come at me, bro). As the story goes, the Martin brothers, streetcar conductors turned restaurant owners in New Orleans in the 1920s, served these sandwiches to their former streetcar coworkers during a strike. Every time a striker would walk into their restaurant, Benny Martin would whisper to his brother, "Here comes another poor boy . . . ," and thus this delightful name wrapped in a class insult was born. History!

Vegetable oil, for frying

RÉMOULADE

1¼ cups mayo

1 large garlic clove, smashed and minced

1 tablespoon prepared horseradish

2 teaspoons whole-grain mustard

1 teaspoon Worcestershire sauce

2 teaspoons hot sauce

2 teaspoons Creole seasoning

1 tablespoon paprika

½ teaspoon cayenne pepper

2 teaspoons pickle juice (dill or sweet, just scoop it out of your pickle jar) (I like sweet) (bread-and-butter pickles are one of my core values)

Salt

SHRIMP

2 pounds peeled and deveined large shrimp

2 tablespoons Creole seasoning

SHRIMP BATTER

1 cup flour

½ cup cornstarch

½ teaspoon baking powder

1 teaspoon cayenne pepper

1 tablespoon onion powder

1 tablespoon garlic powder

2 tablespoons Creole seasoning

1½ cups beer (light- or medium-bodied; I use Shiner Bock, of course!)

SHRIMP BREADING

4 cups panko bread crumbs

THE REST OF IT

8 French rolls

2 or 3 tomatoes, sliced

Thinly sliced iceberg lettuce (RIBBONS of lettuce!)

Pickles

RECIPE CONTINUES

// Preheat your oven to 250°F and set a wire rack on a rimmed baking sheet. Fill your cast-iron skillet, pot, or deep fryer with oil to a depth of 2 inches and heat it up to 350°F. (I like to use my massive cast-iron skillet because I can fry more shrimp at once instead of in 7,000 batches.)

// While that's heating up, throw everything on the rémoulade list into a bowl and whisk to combine. This is all up for grabs. Too tangy? Add mayo. Too flat? Add pickle juice. Too spicy? Go with God. This gets better the longer it sits, so keep it in the fridge for an hour at least, too. Better yet, make it way earlier and tick something off the dinner list.

// Rinse your shrimp, throw it in a bowl, and toss it with the Creole seasoning. Set it aside while you do the next bit. (Do I buy frozen shrimp that has already been cleaned, peeled, and deveined? You know good and damn well I do. If you think I'm going to peel 2 pounds of raw shrimp for this and then still have to BATTER AND FRY IT, you've lost your mind.)

// Whisk everything on the batter list in a bowl, then throw in the shrimp. Let them swim in the batter for 10 minutes or so while you slice the rolls and tomatoes and lettuce.

// Panko time. This is where the crunch factor gets meta. I was going to let this go, but dredging (like an assembly line to batter your shrimp) can turn into a real clumpy shitshow, so here's your trick: Spread a cup or so of the panko in a shallow dish, place your battered shrimp in a single layer on the panko, then just sprinkle more panko over the top. Replenish the bottom layer of panko before each batch. Otherwise, it starts to resemble kitty litter, and now you'll never forget that disgusting comparison. You're welcome.

// As you dredge the shrimp, set them aside on a pan, then fry in batches in the hot oil until golden brown on both sides. This takes anywhere between 3 and 5 minutes. Put each finished batch on the prepared rack and keep them warm in the oven while you fry the rest. (Do you see the dish-and-pan situation I have created for you? It is no joke up in here.)

// **A word about the bread:** If you have room for this in your heart, please get French rolls the Martin brothers would be proud of. Bakery bread, you know what I'm saying? A little chewy on the outside, soft and fluffy on the inside. Don't mess around. Otherwise, putting all this deliciousness on inferior bread is like lipstick on a pig.

// Now build those beautiful sammies. I like rémoulade on the bottom, then tons of shrimp, then more rémoulade, because the only thing better than sauce is more sauce. Pile on the lettuce and tomato slices and pickles. This po'boy is actually too good. It is too sexy for this cookbook.

ALTERNATIVE BATTER
Buttermilk plus Creole seasoning

ALTERNATIVE BREADING
Seasoned cornmeal

ALTERNATIVE SAUCE
Trash Sauce (page 103)

NO-DAMNS ALTERNATIVE
Frozen breaded shrimp

FRIED AVOCADO TACOS

WITH POBLANO RANCH

Before my daughter Sydney became a Chick-fil-A vegetarian (see page 231), when she was just a vegetarian vegetarian, I always cooked alternative dishes for her. I automatically made a small side skillet with no chicken, no beef stock, no sausage, no bacon or whatever. She was out of the house a solid year before I got used to making meat food without a surrogate side piece.

So when I made fried chicken tacos, I had to come up with a Sydney version so she didn't just get a tortilla with lettuce. Vegetarians deserve fried food too, you guys. Non-meat-eaters have the right to high cholesterol as much as the rest of us do. I found this recipe (more or less) via the geniuses at *Bon Appétit*, and it became not only Sydney's equal-but-lesser alternative, but eventually a taco I made for the whole meal. **When delicious things are fried, sometimes your meat-eaters forget to notice they're eating vegetarian.** This sort of trickery will work for even your staunchest cavemen.

POBLANO RANCH

1 poblano pepper

2 scallions, green parts only

¼ cup buttermilk (see Note, page 33)

¼ cup sour cream

¼ cup mayo

Juice of 1 lemon

Salt and pepper

—

6 to 8 flour tortillas

FRIED AVOCADOS

Vegetable or grapeseed oil, for frying

2 firm avocados (not underripe, but not squishy)

2 eggs, beaten

1 cup panko bread crumbs

1 cup flour

2 tablespoons Cajun seasoning

Salt

THE REST OF IT

1 (16-ounce) can refried black beans (A REVELATION)

1 container prepared pico de gallo

Shredded Monterey Jack cheese

2 cups or so ribboned (thin!) iceberg lettuce

// Let's get that poblano roasted for the ranch. Fastest way: Turn your gas burner on high and set your pepper right on the flame. With tongs, turn it about once every 2 minutes until it's blistered on all sides. Or you can do this in a 400°F oven: Toss your pepper in a little bit of oil, throw it on a baking sheet, and roast it for about 20 minutes, turning it every 5 minutes to get all sides blistered. Either way, once it's blackened, put it in a sealed plastic baggie and let it steam for 10 minutes. Take it out, scrape off all the skin with a paring knife, and now you have a perfectly roasted poblano pepper. Put it in your blender with the rest of the ranch ingredients and whiz it up. Keep this in your fridge until it's time to serve.

// Preheat your oven to 300°F. Stack your tortillas, wrap in foil, and throw them in there to warm through until everything else is done.

RECIPE CONTINUES

// Pour about ½ inch of oil into a heavy skillet and heat over medium-high heat while you get those avocados ready. Halve, pit, and peel each one, then cut into 8 wedges per avocado (for 16 wedges total).

// Set up your dredging stations: one shallow dish with the beaten eggs, and a second shallow dish with the panko, flour, and Cajun seasoning. Dunk your avocado wedges into the eggs, then totally coat them with the panko mix. (Panko is the best thing that ever happened to fried food.)

// Add the breaded avocado wedges to the hot oil in a single layer, not touching each other, and fry them, turning with tongs to get all sides brown and crunchy. This will take around 6 to 10 minutes total, depending on your oil, your pan, your weather, and your horoscope. Just make sure you get a nice, brown, crunchy crust on those bad boys. Sprinkle immediately with salt.

// In the meantime, warm your refried black beans in the microwave until nice and steamy. Put a spoon in your store-bought pico. (What? Who cares? Putting a spoon in a container of premade food counts.) Build each taco with the refried beans (or as I like to call them, taco glue) down first, then fried avocado wedges, a drizzle of the poblano ranch, some cheese, lettuce, pico, more ranch. Wait until you bite into that crunchy avocado with this sauce. You'll become a vegetarian for at least the rest of the day.

> ### Note
>
> Any leftover poblano ranch should be drizzled over your eggs the next morning, spooned over your salad, drizzled over roasted veggies, or used as a dip for crudités.

GRILLED PORK BANH MI

The first time I had a banh mi sandwich, I was having lunch with my friend Melissa at Megg's Cafe in Belton, Texas, which makes no sense at all, because:

1. Megg's has things like hash and meatloaf on the menu.
2. Belton is not a mecca of Vietnamese food.
3. Belton is not a mecca of food.

And yet as I live and breathe, that was one of the best sandwiches I have eaten in my existence. I am still talking about it eight years later. I didn't know about banh mi before that day, but then I got my life.

I made these for my girlfriends recently and Jenny was like, "But what are we supposed to do with those sliced raw jalapeños?" and I was like, "Put them on your sandwich and eat them with your mouth," and she was like, "But I can see the seeds in them," and I was all "You are a big girl and you will eat this the proper way," and reader, she DID and immediately repented for doubting the jalapeños and the cook and frankly the entire country of Vietnam.

This is maybe one of the most delicious recipes in this whole book.

PICKLED VEG

1½ cups rice vinegar

1 cup water

¼ cup granulated sugar

2 tablespoons salt

4 ounces shredded carrots (½ cup) (I 100% buy the preshredded bag)

1 bunch radishes, cut into matchsticks (see Note)

MARINATED PORK

½ cup soy sauce

⅓ cup packed brown sugar

3 tablespoons fish sauce

1 lemongrass stalk, bruised with the back of a knife, trimmed, and minced

1 tablespoon minced or grated fresh ginger

5 garlic cloves, chopped

Salt and pepper

1 pound pork tenderloin

FOR SERVING

1 cucumber

1 large or 2 small jalapeños (just do it), sliced (and seeded, if you want a little less ka-POW)

1 bunch cilantro

1 cup mayo

1 tablespoon sriracha

6 soft French rolls

// Now, look, you will do two early things either the night before like a champion or the morning of. Which means come dinnertime, you'll only need around 10 minutes to get this winner on the table.

// **Early Thing #1:** In a container with a lid, whisk together the vinegar, water, granulated sugar, and salt until the sugar and salt have totally dissolved. Add your carrots and radish matchsticks. This is your crunchy pickled veg, and it literally makes the sandwich. Stick it in the fridge.

RECIPE CONTINUES

// **Early Thing #2:** In a baking dish, whisk your marinade ingredients together until incorporated ("soy sauce through salt and pepper"). Trim any fat or membrane off the pork tenderloin and slice it into absolutely razor-thin pieces until you have a whole pile of floppy pork slices. Into the marinade they go. Get them totally coated, cover the baking dish, and stick it in the fridge.

// Now go to bed. Or go about your day. Your work here is done.

// The last four steps take 3 minutes each, so thank earlier you for making this moment possible.

1. Thinly slice your cucumbers and jalapeños, and chop the cilantro.
2. Mix your mayo and sriracha until smooth and set aside.
3. Throw your French rolls into a preheated 350°F oven to get the outsides a little toasty.
4. On a hot grill, cook your marinated pork slices for 2 minutes on each side. That's it. They're done. (You can also just throw these in a hot skillet on your stovetop, but the grill flavor is *chef's kiss.*)

// Build those gorgeous banh mi sammies: huge smear of sriracha mayo on the bottom of each roll, a pile of the marinated pork, tons of pickled veg, fresh cucumber and jalapeño slices, cilantro, one more slather of sriracha mayo on top.

// The minute I finish this sandwich, I want another one.

Note

HOW TO MATCHSTICK RADISHES

Slice off the root end. Carefully slice each radish until you have a pile of thin, round slices (the easiest way to do this is on a mandoline). Then stack a few slices on top of each other and cut them into matchsticks.

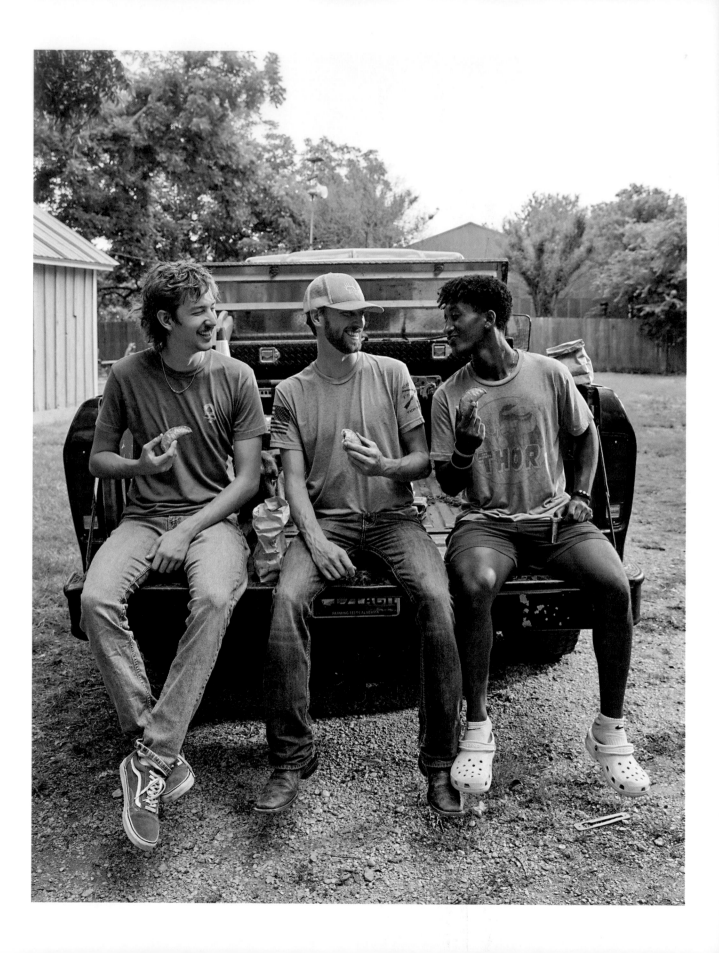

5

FOOD FOR Your PICKY SPOUSE OR SPAWN

UPDATED "KID" RECIPES

HOMEMADE CORN DOGS

AND TRASH SAUCE WITH RELISH

Is there a Sonic in every state in America? My Canadian BFF Sarah *crosses the border* to get their tater tots, and her passport is literally filled with stamps that don't indicate her flair for international travel as much as her obsession with fast-food hash browns. I honor her.

I have three things to mention about Sonic that feel important:

Number one, their ice. Companies actually manufacture ice makers to replicate Sonic's exact "nugget ice" for people who want their pricey pellets. Sure, it may cost more than the free ice in your freezer, but bust out that Sonic ice at your next party, and you can charge per head to recoup the cost. THE PEOPLE WILL PAY IT.

Number two, their mozzarella sticks. I don't care that they come out of a taped box in a subzero freezer with processed honey mustard, I want them now, dammit! I have perfected the mozzarella stick/honey mustard setup in my car's cupholder to still have room for my Diet Dr Pepper while I'm eating with my right hand and driving safely with my left, and now you know I am a leader you can truly look up to.

Number three, their corn dogs. There just truly isn't an equal. I could eat ten in one sitting. They're crunchy and slightly sweet, and on Fridays they're 99 cents. I'll tell you straight up, Sonic lost money on that deal in my zip code. Anyhow, corn dogs are a perfect food and I don't care what anyone says. Make these at home and your kids will think you're cooler than you actually are, and as someone whose favorite show is *CBS Sunday Morning* with Jane Pauley, I say that in solidarity.

High-temp oil (like grapeseed or canola)

—

½ cup flour

1 package all-beef hot dogs (or the garbage ones, which are, unfortunately, delicious)

BATTER

1 (8.5-ounce) box sweet cornbread (or honey cornbread) mix

½ cup flour

1 tablespoon sweet paprika

1 teaspoon salt

½ teaspoon cayenne pepper (optional) ("some like it hot, so let's turn up the heat till we fry")

1 cup milk, plus more if needed

TRASH SAUCE WITH RELISH

¼ cup ketchup

½ cup mayo

3 tablespoons mustard

3 tablespoons relish (dill or sweet)

// LOL on this recipe. Look, you turned to the chapter on picky eaters, so this is what you get, because the number of people who don't like corn dogs is zero. Don't act shocked that I'm giving you hot dogs and something called "Trash Sauce."

// Preheat your oven to 250°F and set a wire rack on a rimmed baking sheet. Pour 2 inches of oil into your pot and heat over medium-high heat. (Make sure the pot is wide enough to handle the length of the hot dogs.) (Hold the dirty jokes, you gutter brains.)

// Put the flour in a zip-top bag, add the hot dogs, and shake to coat. Otherwise, your fancy batter will slide right off those bad boys.

// Mix the batter ingredients in a shallow dish with a whisk. You want this to look slightly thicker than pancake batter. Add more milk if it's too thick.

// Using tongs, shake off the excess flour from each hot dog, give them a good dunk in the batter, making sure to get each one fully coated, and put them carefully into the hot oil, working in batches to avoid crowding them. After 2 or 3 minutes, flip them and fry until they're totally brown and dreamy. Pull them out of the hot oil with your tongs, set them on the rack, and keep them warm in the oven until the rest are finished.

// Mix all the Trash Sauce ingredients in a bowl until smooth.

// Spear each hot dog with a wooden skewer and serve them with the Trash Sauce in little individual dip bowls, which is a Mom Hack for getting kids to eat things. But dip bowls or not, your little piggies will gobble these up. Sonic? YOU'VE BEEN SERVED, SON.

Chicken Potpie

My brother, Drew, maintains that one time, Mom made him eat chicken potpie from Sam's Club and he threw it up and could not eat a bite of it again for twenty years, and Mom categorically denies this because she says she never bought chicken potpie from Sam's in her life and that she would know because she is the person who actually shopped for our food and he was just a dumb kid making up fake childhood memories, but this is Drew's truth and now you know the story of our family chicken potpie drama.

Because Drew and his wife, Sarah, and my nephews live 4 minutes from my house, I lure them over at least two nights a week with the low-hanging fruit of Free-and-Already-Fixed Dinner, because what full-time working parents with babies want by day's end is an overinvested sister/SIL/aunt prepared to bribe them with food. I already had this dish in the oven the night Drew told me about his CPP horror, but I fed him this exact recipe and he ate two giant servings, so apparently trauma can be overcome with time and perseverance and homemade food that didn't come from a bulk store where you get your toilet paper.

4 tablespoons (½ stick) butter

½ cup diced onion

½ cup diced carrots

½ cup diced celery

—

3 to 4 cups shredded cooked chicken (you know I use a rotisserie chicken)

2 garlic cloves, chopped

⅓ cup flour

3 cups chicken stock, plus more if needed

⅓ cup dry white wine (I guess you'll have to drink the rest of the bottle)

1 tablespoon chopped fresh thyme

Salt and pepper

⅓ cup heavy cream

1 cup frozen peas

—

1 (2-count) package store-bought rolled pie crusts (no shame in my game)

—

1 egg, beaten

// Preheat your oven to 375°F.

// In a Dutch oven or other large pot, melt the butter over medium heat, then add the onion, carrots, and celery and cook, stirring frequently, until your veggies are just softened but not browned, maybe 5 minutes. **(This irreplaceable flavor base is called a mirepoix—that's MEER-pwah—and it is the start of one million good things. At all times, have these items on hand, home cook.)**

// Throw in your chicken, garlic, flour, stock, wine, thyme, and salt and pepper to taste. Stir until the mixture is totally incorporated and thickening up, 5 minutes or so. Stir in the cream and peas and cook for another minute. I loooooooooove peas. Love love love. Grab a quick taste and see if you'd like to adjust any of the seasonings or liquids (you can add more stock if it seems too dry). It is very possible to underseason chicken potpie filling, so make sure you have enough salt and pepper.

// On to the crust. I am an evangelist for top AND bottom crusts for chicken potpie. Sandwiching that delicious chicken mixture between two browned, crunchy crusts is the business. With such devotion, you'd think I'd make my own crusts, but you would be wrong. Adjust your opinion of me accordingly.

// Roll out one crust and transfer it to a 9-inch pie dish, pressing it over the bottom and up the sides and letting the excess hang over the edge. Carefully pour in the chicken mixture, making sure it isn't spilling over. Roll out the second crust and lay it over the top. Crimp the edges together any which random way to seal the deal. I hate when people say to trim the excess crust, because all that does is get rid of the best part. Just squeeze it all into submission. All crust, all day.

// Make a few slits in the top with a knife and brush the beaten egg all over the top and edges. This needs to bake for 30 minutes, but the edges of the crust always get a little burny, so crimp some foil around just the edges for either the first 10 minutes or the last 10 minutes so they don't overdo. If you can find it in your heart, let the potpie sit for 10 minutes before serving so it doesn't run all over your plate or sear the roof of your mouth to death.

// This will not cause your children an ounce of trauma. They will tell no lies about your bulk grocery store chicken potpies.

Quesadillas, Three Ways

It's like this: I will eat absolutely anything you stick between two tortillas and grill. I have literally never had a quesadilla I didn't love, and I've eaten some weird ones. This is a fantastic way to introduce new flavors and ingredients to your picky kids because they can't see them. Joke's on you, clowns. You don't "like" roasted red peppers, my ass.

Every one of these is foolproof. They taste delicious, they come with dips, and they are melty. What else could these people possibly want from us? Figure one quesadilla per person (or two, if your people are teen boys). You can use a skillet, but a griddle is tons faster because you can cook three or four at once.

PER QUESADILLA

2 large flour tortillas

1 tablespoon butter or oil

HAWAIIAN QUESADILLAS

PER QUESADILLA

½ to 1 cup shredded Monterey Jack cheese

2 tablespoons barbecue sauce

½ to 1 cup shredded cooked chicken

¼ cup crumbled cooked bacon

¼ cup chopped pineapple (fresh or canned in juice)

1 to 2 tablespoons finely diced fresh jalapeño

1 to 2 tablespoons finely diced red onion

Salt and pepper

// The key to that quesadilla life is cheese on the bottom, cheese on top. This keeps the filling in quesadilla prison where it belongs, instead of trying to escape. So, for each quesadilla: Spread half your Monterey Jack on one tortilla, drizzle evenly with barbecue sauce, then top with the chicken, bacon, pineapple, jalapeño, and onion and sprinkle with salt and pepper. Finish with the rest of the cheese again and the top tortilla. Give the stack a good press with your spatula so all that stuff wants to stay inside.

// Melt the butter on your griddle or in a skillet over medium heat, then grill your quesadillas on the first side for 3 minutes or so (check for toasty brown on the bottom). Carefully flip, add a bit more butter, and grill until the quesadillas are browned and crunchy on the second side and the cheese is gooey. Absolutely delicious.

// Remove from the pan and let your quesadillas sit for a couple of minutes before you cut them into quarters so the innards don't just ooze out. My kids dip Hawaiian quesadillas in ranch, which makes absolutely no sense, but here we are.

RECIPE CONTINUES

CHORIZO, REFRIED BEAN, AND CHEDDAR QUESADILLAS
WITH SCALLION-AVOCADO SOUR CREAM

1 pound ground chorizo

1 (16-ounce) can refried beans

1 cup chopped pickled jalapeños

1 cup chopped onion

2 to 3 cups shredded cheddar cheese (8 to 12 ounces)

SCALLION-AVOCADO SOUR CREAM

1 cup sour cream

1 avocado, diced

1 tomato, diced

3 tablespoons chopped scallion

1 teaspoon ground cumin

Salt

// Brown your chorizo in a skillet over medium heat, then remove from the heat and drain off the fat. Warm up your refried beans in the microwave like the culinary school students do. Then just mix the chorizo and refried beans in a bowl. This is excellent quesadilla glue, too.

// Down on each bottom tortilla: chorizo-and-bean combo, jalapeños, onion, cheese, then add the top tortilla. My son Caleb's favorite food is raw onion, so we love its sweet crunch. Plus, raw onion on beany, meaty food makes me think of Taco Bell. (And when I say "think," I mean WITH GREAT FONDNESS. My stars, the WAY I love Taco Bell. If you wouldn't go facedown in a Mexican Pizza with Fire Sauce, I don't know why you bother eating any food at all.)

// Heat your butter or oil over medium heat on your griddle or skillet over medium heat, then grill the quesadillas until toasty brown, around 3 minutes per side.

// Mix together all the stuff for the scallion-avocado sour cream and dollop it on top of your delicious quesadillas. There is a 0% chance your people won't love this.

SHRIMP AND PEPPER JACK QUESADILLAS
WITH BANG BANG SAUCE

BANG BANG SAUCE

½ cup mayo

1 to 2 tablespoons sriracha, to taste

1 tablespoon rice vinegar

1 tablespoon fresh lime juice

Dash of sugar, to taste

Dash of salt, to taste

SHRIMP

1 pound peeled and deveined shrimp

Salt and black pepper

1 tablespoon red pepper flakes

2 tablespoons olive oil

——

2 to 3 cups shredded pepper Jack cheese (8 to 12 ounces)

1 (12-ounce) jar roasted red peppers, drained and chopped

1 bunch cilantro, chopped

// Preheat your oven to 400°F.

// Mix all your Bang Bang Sauce stuff together and stick it in the fridge so the flavors can start getting serious with each other. Let them get to second base. Then, as always, taste and adjust.

// Meanwhile, toss the shrimp, some salt and black pepper, the red pepper flakes, and the olive oil on a baking sheet and roast for 7 to 10 minutes (start checking the shrimp at 7 minutes—when they're done, they should look opaque). Roasted shrimp is a revelation I learned from Ina. Somehow, Ina knows everything. This earth is her kingdom and we are just her serfs.

// After the shrimp cools for a minute or two, chop it into smaller pieces. Layer up your quesadilla: cheese, red peppers, diced shrimp, cilantro, more cheese. Grill on both sides until toasty and melty, about 3 minutes per side. Let each one cool a few minutes, cut into quarters, and drizzle with the Bang Bang Sauce. Come on. You know this is good. Make this immediately.

Potato Chip, Bacon, and Raspberry Grilled Cheese

This is exactly what it sounds like, and listen up, folx, I am a grown adult lady and I put potato chips on my sandwich every day. I'm just out here trying to do better, and crunchy salty chips on a sandwich is how to level up your life. So is this entire sammie of wonderment.

I've been at this parenting gig for almost a quarter century, and I've discovered that sandwiches and tortillas and pasta are reliable coconspirators in getting your people to try new things. *What? Those green stalky things? Who cares! They're buried in a creamy pasta! Those peas? Are like little green candies! Eat up, kiddies!*

Also, now that I'm watching my brother and sister-in-law feed their boys flavorful, grown-up food from the time they cut their first teeth, I want a redo. To be fair, my kids got stupid brown freezer food when they were little because I didn't even know you could buy whole garlic and thought salmon came in shelf-stable tins. I thought children only ate dinosaur-shaped chicken nuggets and the outer limits of their flavor profile was ketchup. My babies were effed.

I eventually fixed them when I started cooking, but I had to sneak in a bunch of stuff for a while. I am pleased to report that every one of my kids would squeeze sriracha right into their mouth hole as a snack now, so take heart! Kids *can* become good eaters who don't order "noodles with butter" for $9.99 at Olive Garden.

I'm a recent convert to the mayo-instead-of-butter-outer-slather on grilled cheese. Y'all: DELIGHTFUL. Because I am so extra, I tried a butter-mayo combo, died, and went straight to heaven. This is my ghost writing. I am an angel now. So mix the two, and that's what you're going to slather on the outside of your sandwiches before you grill.

Sourdough: Levels up your grilled cheese.
Shredded Gruyère: Levels up your grilled cheese.
Bacon: Levels up your grilled cheese.
Raspberry jam: Levels up your grilled cheese.
Potato chips: I mean, get out of here.

This is the perfect flavor combination: salty, creamy, sweet, and crunchy. Every bite makes you wish you had two mouths.

RECIPE CONTINUES

½ cup (1 stick) butter, at room temp

½ cup mayo

FOR EACH SAMMIE

2 slices sourdough bread

1 to 2 tablespoons raspberry jam (if your peeps are weird about seeds, use strawberry jam)

One layer of thick potato chips (like kettle chips)

2 bacon slices, cooked until crisp

⅓ cup shredded Gruyère cheese (1.5 ounces)

// In a small bowl, mix together your butter and mayo. You'll have about a cup, which is enough for slathering about 4 sandwiches. If you don't use it all, cover it and keep it in the fridge for up to 3 days to use for another batch later.

// In between your slices of sourdough, get generous with a base layer of raspberry jam, then a layer of chips, then the bacon, and finally the shredded Gruyère on top. If you like to live right on the edge, finish with another layer of jam. Before you butter-mayo the outsides, give this a little press to crunch those chips down and keep your sammie together.

// Slather one side with the butter-mayo and put it facedown in a skillet or on a griddle over medium heat. Slather the top with the butter-mayo while it grills. Flip it when the first side is brown and toasty, after 3 minutes or so. When it is a crunchy miracle on both sides and the cheese is oozing, it's time to party.

PECAN-CRUSTED Chicken Strips WITH Honey Dijonnaise

I've given you plenty of fried food in this cookbook, so you know I'm not precious, but frying food is literally a hot mess and it makes my hair smell like oil for four days (which is how long I go without washing my hair). The problem is that I like crunchy food. The other problem is that I love chicken strips like a true child of the '80s indoctrinated by Tyson. So what is a girl to do when she wants her crispy strips but doesn't want to wipe down every kitchen surface with bleach water like she's running a Popeyes?

She makes this recipe, is what she does.

(Very briefly, about Popeyes: I ate my first spicy chicken sandwich from Popeyes during the Pandemic That Would Never End, and that sandwich immediately became my spiritual director. I am furious at every one of you who never told me to eat at Popeyes. Almost every employee is chronically angry, and one time a drive-through cashier in Birmingham told me she "didn't have time for my mess," which only made me love her and the sandwich more. I am a Popeyes evangelist.)

Nonstick cooking spray

HONEY DIJONNAISE

½ cup mayo

2 tablespoons Dijon mustard

1 tablespoon honey

Pinch of salt

—

1 to 2 pounds chicken strips (or cut 3 or 4 breasts into strips with your own damn hands)

1 tablespoon salt

1 tablespoon pepper

—

1 (6-ounce) bag pecans (or honey-roasted pecans, if you love a touch of sweet with your savory) (¾ cup)

1 to 2 tablespoons Cajun seasoning

1 cup panko bread crumbs

2 tablespoons dried parsley

—

2 eggs, beaten

1 tablespoon milk

// Preheat your oven to 400°F and spray a baking sheet with nonstick spray. Last time I made this, I was out of Pam, so I just drizzled grapeseed oil all over my baking sheet, and that works, too. We're basically going to be light-frying/heavy-baking in our ovens, which is superior to stovetop frying because ovens can get splattery and gross but we don't have to look at them like we do our countertops. **All ovens are clean! Because they are closed!**

// In a bowl, mix all the ingredients for the honey Dijonnaise until smooth, then stick it in the fridge.

// Pat your chicken strips dry and sprinkle them with the salt and pepper.

// In your food processor, whiz up the pecans, Cajun seasoning, panko, and parsley (or pulse them in your blender, or chop everything with a knife like our foremothers). You don't want big chunks of pecans because they don't stick as well, so process this into a pretty fine breading.

// Set up your dredging stations: Put your beaten eggs and milk in one shallow dish (I always use pie plates for dredging) and the breading mix in another. In batches, dunk your chicken strips first into the egg mixture, then into the breading, making sure to get them good and coated on all sides. Place the strips in a single layer (not touching) on your prepared baking sheet as you go.

// Bake for around 20 minutes, flipping each strip over at the halfway mark to get both sides crunchy brown. To test for doneness, cut into the thickest strip and check the center—there should be no pink.

// These chicken strips are simply delicious dunked into the honey Dijonnaise. Crunchy outside, tender inside, yummy creamy dip. If your picky eaters don't love these, I will drive to your house and put them in time-out myself. I swear to the Lord.

KIRK'S MOM'S Spiced Jamaican Patties

Over a decade ago, I was at my friends Kirk and T's house while Kirk's mom, who grew up in Spanish Town, Jamaica, was visiting. She'd been rolling and cooking and crimping and baking, and the next thing I knew, I was eating a handheld spiced meat pie that was so delicious, I became its instant disciple. An on-the-spot convert. And if you think I'm kidding, I made such a nuisance of myself about that spiced patty that one time, Kirk brought me back a batch from her house in a brown paper bag. FROM FLORIDA. When a grown man carries a bag of his mom's homemade stuffed pastries on a three-hour flight for his friend, you know that friend's been insufferable.

It should be obvious why your family will love these. This is the Jamaican version of empanadas, or calzones, or samosas, or spanakopita, or, hell, McDonald's apple pies. **The whole world knows to put yummy fillings inside dough and bake it.** The novelty of a personal handheld pie will 100% work on your kids, and the deliciousness will convert them forever.

I wish you could've experienced these at Nice Mon, Kirk's mom's restaurant in Florida, but guess what? You can make them yourself. When I originally asked T to finagle the recipe for me, she said, "You know, all good Jamaican cooks say 'Just a scoop of lard will do, no need to measure.'" Half this ingredient list is just spices. You don't call something a "spiced Jamaican patty" without spices, so jot that down.

Nonstick cooking spray

1 (2-count) package store-bought rolled pie crusts (and? so?)

—

2 tablespoons butter

1 tablespoon olive oil

1 tablespoon curry powder

1 tablespoon ground allspice

Salt and pepper

1 onion, chopped

1 habanero chile, seeded and minced (Got kitchen gloves? Wear them while handling!)

4 scallions, chopped

1 tablespoon chopped fresh thyme

—

1 pound 85% lean ground beef

—

¼ cup bread crumbs

½ cup beef stock

—

2 eggs, beaten

// Yes, I am giving you store-bought pie crust. You're welcome. Honestly, the filling is the star, and the pastry is the stage mom. The filling always eclipses her and she is just going to have to work out her unrealized dreams in therapy.

// Preheat your oven to 400°F and spray a baking sheet with nonstick spray.

// Let's get that pie crust ready. Which is to say, roll both crusts out on a floured surface to about ⅛ inch thick, then cut out eight 5-inch circles total. (I'm not trying to brag, but my store-bought pie crust package comes automatically with two. Use them both, because these patties freeze beautifully.) Stick your crust rounds in the fridge to firm up while you move on to the spiced beef.

RECIPE CONTINUES

// In a skillet, heat the butter and oil over medium heat, then add the curry powder, allspice, and some salt and black pepper. Stir until the spices are toasted and incorporated. (Infusing your butter and oil with spices is a pro move.) Add the onion, habanero, scallions, and thyme and sauté until the veggies start to soften, around 4 minutes. Add the ground beef and stir until it is totally browned, about 5 minutes. Throw in the bread crumbs and stock and cook until the liquid has mostly evaporated, 6 to 8 minutes. This should be perfectly saucy but not soupy.

// Kirk's mom sticks this whole mix in the freezer for 15 minutes both to cool it sufficiently and to hustle the fat to the surface so she can skim it off. (Fun tip: You can also make this filling the day before or morning of and keep it covered in the fridge until you need it.)

// **Let's fill those crusts:** Spoon 2 to 3 tablespoons of the filling onto one half of each pastry round. Moisten the edges of the pastry with a little water and fold in half, totally enclosing the filling. Crimp the edges with a fork to seal. Aren't they darling??? Set the filled patties on your prepared baking sheet and brush each with beaten egg for the most perfect crust.

// Bake for about 30 minutes, until golden brown. Trust your friend Jen when I say to let these gorgeous little babies cool for 5 to 10 minutes before biting into one. I understand your enthusiasm. I ate a bag of these straight out of an airplane overhead bin.

// Thank you, Kirk's mom!

// Thank you, Jamaica!

Note

These would be absolutely delicious with a chimichurri. You could also pair it with zhoug (see page 171), which is similar.

DiNer CHEESEBURGER SLiDERS

WITH Hot Trash Sauce

HOT TRASH SAUCE

¼ cup mayo

1 tablespoon Dijon mustard

2 tablespoons ketchup

1 tablespoon hot sauce

Pinch of salt

SLIDERS

1 pound 80% lean ground beef (if your 95% lean burgers come out bad, don't cry to me)

2 tablespoons Worcestershire sauce

1 teaspoon salt

Uncle Chris' Gourmet Steak Seasoning (this is worth your online order)

TO ASSEMBLE AND SERVE

Sliced sharp cheddar cheese (or whatever cheese you loooooove)

Hawaiian slider rolls

Butter

Pickles (dill or bread-and-butter)

Look, do you want to be precious about it, or do you want to eat the most delicious cheeseburger slider in North America? Don't get me wrong, I'll eat a fancy grilled burger with roasted chanterelles or whatever all the livelong day, but what people really want is a nod to those 1:30 a.m. Waffle House runs after going hard where no one has ever said the word "chanterelle" but they have very much said the words "smoking allowed."

I need to give credit here, because one time, the weirdest thing ever happened: I found myself at Willie Robertson's house (of *Duck Dynasty* fame), and he made these "Willie Burgers," which seemed very . . . unlike the way we cooked burgers. Super-thin patties, fried on a hot griddle, tented with cheese, and very unadorned. I looked at his wife, Korie, skeptically, and she said, "Just eat it." I did. And let me tell you something: joy to the whole wide world. So this is my take on the Willie Burger, which goes to show you that you can have polar opposite ideologies on gun control and political parties but identical values on fried cheeseburgers. BIPARTISANSHIP LIVES.

This serves six. Double it if you're feeding the Hatmakers.

// No need to fire up the grill, because these babies are going on the griddle. You are engineering your own personal Waffle House tonight, honey bunny. I use a cast-iron griddle and lay it across two burners. You could also use a wide, flat-bottomed skillet. Either way, fire up your griddle or pan over medium-high heat until it's nice and hot. These sliders are going to fry in their own grease and you are not going to fuss about that.

// Throw all the Hot Trash Sauce ingredients into a bowl, mix, and set aside.

// For the sliders, mix the ground beef, Worcestershire, and salt by hand in a bowl. Form the mixture into 12 small, slider-size patties and—this is important—make them thin. We are not, I repeat, *not* doing big thick juicy burgers. Think less "steak house" and more "McDonald's."

// Now, here in Texas, Uncle Chris' Gourmet Steak Seasoning is as much a staple as bread or milk. You can go on the World Wide Web and order it for $3.25, and I am telling you, a 401(k) isn't a better investment. However, if this feels too hard, replace it with any steak seasoning and everyone will live. Sprinkle both sides of each patty with Uncle Chris' or your inferior steak seasoning.

RECIPE CONTINUES

// Onto the griddle. These should absolutely sizzle and pop and make a giant mess of your stovetop. This is how you know you're doing it right. We want these seared nice and brown on the first side, which takes 2 to 4 minutes. Flip, cover with cheddar, and cook for 2 to 3 more minutes. If you feel like it, tent the pan with foil or a metal bowl to melt that cheese lickety-split.

// Meanwhile, slice your slider buns and butter each side. Save some room on the griddle, and just before serving, brown the buns in the meat juice, buttered-side down. You already know this is going to taste delicious.

// We aren't getting fancy here. The perfect combination: big dollop of Trash Sauce on the bottom bun, thin griddled cheeseburger (or make it a double if you're in it to win it), pickles, one more dollop of Trash Sauce, top bun. This is the end of the story. These are a MESS to eat with their delightful drippy juices and sloppy sauce. If these sliders can bridge the gap between the Second Amendment 'Merica First crowd and the loosey-goosey bleeding-heart lefty libs, we should elect them to Congress and finally achieve world peace. These taste so freakishly good, I would sit in a deer blind just to thank Willie for the inspiration.

> ## Note
>
> Serve these with Perfect Onion Rings (page 237), and you'll never make a different dinner.

6

FOOD *FOR* HIPPIES

VEGETARIAN & VEGAN RECIPES

Tray's Tomato Pie

Tray and Jenny have been my best friends since 1998 and live forty-five seconds from my doorstep. When I went through an unexpected divorce in 2020 (may its memory burn in all our hells), I told Tray and Jenny I was married to them now, because we've been friends longer than most marriages, so we were going to celebrate our anniversary and make life decisions together, and Tray started a group text with me and Jenny and named it "thruple."

In addition to being my thruple husband, Tray has some other proclivities that belie his 300-pound, former-Alabama-offensive-lineman frame. The first has to do with hummingbirds, and I'll just say that no large human man has ever been more invested in the feeding and watching of hummingbirds off his deck, nor demonstrated such animosity toward the squirrels that steal their sugar water. Year after year with the hummingbirds, man. Us wives never hear the end of it.

The second has to do with fresh summer tomatoes. Tray has driven 90 miles round trip just to get a brown paper bag of fresh produce from his "tomato guy." We share a radical love of summer tomatoes, so he always brings me a few because he'll get the reaction he wants (second wives in a thruple can delight over small gestures, while first/actual wives are like, *so help me Oprah, if I have to hear about the damn hummingbirds another minute . . .*).

Not surprisingly, Tray makes the most delicious tomato pie in the United States of America, and if you've never had tomato pie, get ready to live.

2 larger or 3 smaller ripe red farmer-worthy tomatoes

Salt

—

1 store-bought rolled pie crust (I don't care)

—

⅔ cup mayo

8 ounces shredded sharp cheddar cheese (1 cup)

4 ounces grated Parmesan cheese (½ cup)

¼ cup chopped scallions

1 jalapeño, seeded and finely diced

—

Pepper

// Preheat your oven to 425°F.

// Let's quick prep those tomatoes. Slice your 'maters, place them in a single layer over a blanket of paper towels, and sprinkle them evenly with salt. Let them sit there and leach off a bit of their moisture while you do the rest. Tomatoes vary wildly in size, so you might use all of these slices, or you might not. (If you have extra slices at the end, make a tomato sandwich, which Tray makes with just white bread and mayonnaise. What on earth.)

// Of course you could make a homemade pie crust, which is exactly what my grandma Fay King would do if she was alive. So would my former mother-in-law, Jacki; my sis-in-law Lana; my mom, Jana, between 1985 and 1995 (now she doesn't give a damn); and all my cookbook writer friends. Again, they handed a cookbook contract to someone who puts "store-bought pie crust" on the ingredient list, which proves that sometimes good things happen to mediocre people.

// Press your pie crust into a 9-inch pie pan, crimping the edges however which way, and bake for 5 minutes. Remove the crust from the oven and lower the oven temp to 375°F.

// In the meantime, mix the mayo, cheddar, Parmesan, scallions, and jalapeño in a bowl. **A word: I feel unreasonably strongly about shredding your own cheese, with almost no exceptions.** Since I've instructed you to use a store-bought crust, you know I am not precious, but we simply cannot compare block cheese to bagged preshredded cheese. We shan't. The preshredded stuff is coated with weirdness and it 100% affects your recipes for the worse. Some shortcuts I wholeheartedly endorse, but bagged cheese is not one of them, and if you insist on using it here, I want you to sign a waiver acknowledging that your tomato pie will be the lesser for it.

// Layer your delicious sliced tomatoes evenly over the bottom of the pie crust, overlapping them slightly so they cover the bottom completely but don't take up any more pie real estate, then sprinkle evenly with pepper, since you've already salted them. Spread the cheese mixture evenly over the tomatoes.

// Bake for 30 minutes, or until the tomato pie is bubbling and starting to brown a bit. Check it at 20 minutes, and if it is starting to brown too much, loosely cover it with foil until the end. Ovens are weird and need to be babysat through new recipes.

// Let the pie cool for 10 minutes before absolutely devouring this little bit of summer heaven. Wondering if you're supposed to eat this for breakfast, brunch, lunch, or dinner? Yes. My thruple will be eating this on our next anniversary while we discuss our retirement plans.

Veggie Gratin

I grew up eating vegetables during the '80s, and it was a real culinary tragedy. As far as we could tell, vegetables came out of cans, and if they were fancy (frozen), we ate them after they were boiled into mush. If you haven't ever eaten Brussels sprouts boiled to death in plain water, then I guess your mom didn't hate you. We were warriors for choking that mess down back when moms didn't make three separate meals for their snowflakes' personal preferences. Moms were like, "Eat that broccoli now or you will damn well eat it cold for breakfast tomorrow, and my morning playlist will be the sound of your tears."

I am just saying that '80s food put a lot of us in therapy, but when we know better, we do better, and you can get your kids to eat any single vegetable (or combination of veggies) if you cook it like this. **I usually pick whatever is on its last living leg in my vegetable drawer.** I have made this with every veggie that exists, and there is no loser, because when you put enough butter, cheese sauce, and toasted bread crumbs on something, it tastes good. We didn't have this masterful approach back in the day. Thanks a lot, Communism.

Nonstick cooking spray

3 tablespoons olive oil

3 tablespoons butter

8 cups chopped or thinly sliced veggie (any, or a combo)

1 onion, diced

3 or 4 garlic cloves, minced

1 tablespoon seasoning blend (Creole, jerk, Mediterranean, Italian, whatever you like)

Salt and black pepper

CHEESE SAUCE

2 tablespoons butter

2 tablespoons flour

2 cups milk or half-and-half

1 teaspoon ground nutmeg

Pinch of cayenne pepper

1 tablespoon whole-grain mustard

Salt and black pepper

1 cup grated cheese (I love Gruyère, but cheddar is also delish) (4 ounces)

TOPPING

½ cup bread crumbs

2 tablespoons butter, melted

—

Chopped fresh parsley, for garnish (optional)

// First of all, yes, this calls for 7 tablespoons of butter, but did I or did I not tell you I was going to get your people to eat any vegetable that exists? How else do you think that happens?

// Preheat your oven to 350°F and spray a 9 x 13-inch baking dish with nonstick spray.

// In a large skillet, heat the olive oil and butter over medium-high heat, then add your sliced veggie, onion, garlic, seasoning, and salt and pepper and sauté until the vegetables are tender, around 10 minutes (longer for sturdier veggies like potatoes or Brussels sprouts).

// Meanwhile, on to the béchamel cheese sauce, which is what you are making. Congratulations on being a French chef. In a separate pan, melt the butter over medium heat, then whisk in the flour and cook, whisking, for 2 to 3 minutes, until the flour is incorporated and starting to brown. Whisk in the milk, nutmeg, cayenne, mustard, and salt and black pepper until the sauce is smooth and creamy. Babysit this with your whisk as it cooks until it starts to thicken, about 5 minutes. Take it off the heat and stir in the cheese.

RECIPE CONTINUES

// (Excuse me, but now that you know how to make this béchamel cheese sauce, do note that it can be the star of any pasta, lasagna, fondue, mac and cheese, tuna bake, scalloped potatoes, moussaka, rice, or chicken bake. It is delicious 100% of the time, and everybody loves it. You could drizzle this over Brussels sprouts boiled to death in plain water and your family would still ask for seconds.)

// Transfer the sautéed veggies to your prepared baking dish, then pour the cheese sauce evenly over everything. Sprinkle the bread crumbs evenly over the top, then drizzle with the melted butter. Bake for about 25 minutes, until the top is crunchy toasty brown and the sauce is bubbling.

// If you like, sprinkle parsley over the whole thing before serving. Of course this is delicious. I mean, read the recipe. If my mom fed us vegetables like this in 1986, it probably would've changed the course of my life, because worth admitting is that until I taught myself to cook, I boiled canned green beans for my kids and melted two slices of American cheese on top, so generational trauma is real. If they write a snarky cookbook one day and talk about the Green Beans and Kraft Cheese Slices Tragedy, I will tear this page out and mail it to them until they take that shit back.

Awesome veggie choices
for gratin:

+ **Cauliflower**

+ **Broccoli**

+ **Zucchini**

+ **Summer squash**

+ **Tomatoes**

+ **Butternut squash**

+ **Kale**

+ **Potatoes**

+ **Spinach and leeks**

+ **Parsnips**

+ **Brussels sprouts**

"Noodles"
with Crispy Broccoli
and Cashew Cream Sauce

One time I was doing this wretched "no dairy, sugar, gluten, or alcohol" thing for a month because I don't know why. I love those categories. Gluten is my favorite food. Anyhow, the only thing worse than deprivation is bland food. Like, if you tell me to eat steamed broccoli with plain chicken, we are going to come to fisticuffs. So I was determined to cook dishes that tasted like something.

Scouring the internet for other dum-dums making compliant recipes, I came across this one. In my life, I have never rolled my eyes so hard. They literally called it "Pasta with Alfredo Sauce," but I learned to read when I was four, so I could plainly see that zucchini noodles are not "pasta" and cashew cream sauce is I don't even know what but it sure as hell isn't "Alfredo." But I was so desperate for something creamy that I decided to waste $9.99 on a package of whole raw cashews on the off chance that this recipe wasn't stupid (but on the likely chance that I could talk shit about it on the internet).

Reader, I took one bite and burst out laughing. It was so delicious, I was actually furious. The vegans, man. Their quest to take over the world is well in hand. I've tweaked and tweaked this, and here's my favorite version. You're going to love it. Make your peace.

Here are several options for your "noodles," in descending order by fuss factor:

1. **Spaghetti squash:** Cut 2 spaghetti squash in half lengthwise, scoop out the seeds, drizzle with olive oil, roast flesh-side down at 375°F for 45 minutes, then shred with a fork into "noodles." It does this. I don't know what to say. It is a magic vegetable. Season with salt and pepper.

2. **Zucchini** (you'll need 3) **or butternut squash** (just 1): Use a spiralizer to crank out your own "noodles." Just before serving, sauté your zoodles (ugh) in 2 tablespoons olive oil over medium heat for 2 minutes. Season with salt and pepper.

3. Buy a 24-ounce package **spiralized zucchini or butternut squash noodles** from your produce department, because we can't care about everything. Sauté in 2 tablespoons olive oil over medium heat for 2 minutes. Season with salt and pepper.

4. (If you don't give a damn about gluten, you can obviously serve this over your favorite **gluten-full noodles**.)

CASHEW CREAM SAUCE

12 ounces raw cashews

1 (13.5-ounce) can full-fat coconut milk

13.5 ounces veggie stock (just use the empty coconut milk can to measure)

Juice of 1 big lemon

1 teaspoon salt

2 garlic cloves, peeled

A few dashes of cayenne pepper

A few dashes of freshly grated nutmeg

CRISPY BROCCOLI

4 tablespoons coconut oil (vegan), or 2 tablespoons coconut oil plus 2 tablespoons butter (like our grandmas)

4 cups coarsely chopped broccoli florets

1 teaspoon salt

3 garlic cloves, chopped

1 tablespoon red pepper flakes

A good squeeze of lemon juice

—

Veggie "noodles" (any of the options described above)

Black pepper

RECIPE CONTINUES

// The people who make up food like this say to soak your cashews first, so combine all the cashew cream ingredients in a blender and just leave it sitting there, unblended, for 30 minutes while you do the other stuff. Then blend it all up on the highest setting for 3 minutes to pulverize those cashews into a smooth sauce so it won't be gritty.

// This will make more sauce than you need (it's hard to halve because of the coconut milk), so save the leftovers to drizzle over roasted veggies, spoon over a hearty salad, use as a dip for crudités, dollop on baked potatoes, mix with rice, or use as a white pizza sauce. Yum!

// Meanwhile, in a big skillet, melt 2 tablespoons of the coconut oil over high heat, add the broccoli, and sauté for around 5 minutes so it sears nice and crispy. Don't stir it too much. Let it brown! Season with the salt. Turn down the heat to medium, and add 2 tablespoons more coconut oil (or 2 tablespoons butter), the garlic, red pepper flakes, and lemon juice. Cook for 2 more minutes.

// In the big skillet, mix your noodles, broccoli, and cashew cream until the sauce is warmed through. If the sauce is a little thick, just add hot water a tablespoon at a time until you like the consistency. Absolutely douse this with fresh pepper.

// Although I initially had to hard sell the weirdo vegan cashew fake pasta dish, EVERY.SINGLE.KID asks for seconds when I make this. The broccoli florets become little sponges for all that sauce, and you'll love it. I don't care what you say.

Note

Not a vegetarian? This is delicious with shredded chicken or roasted shrimp.

SWEET POTATO AND BLACK BEAN
BuRGeRS

I am already mad at you in advance for skipping this recipe because it's vegetarian. I AM A BURGER ELITIST, and I would never give you a stupid burger. You are going to make this vegetarian burger (fine, it's vegan, RELAX), and you are going to love it, and your family is going to love it, and you will be sorry you didn't trust me.

I workshopped this burger a hundred times when my daughter Sydney became a vegetarian, because (ham)burgers are my favorite thing, but making a whole alternative burger for one person is dumb. So I was determined to fine-tune a veggie burger that my feminist, liberal, gay vegetarian would love; that my gun-toting, ranch-management-major son would love; that my libertarian, conspiracy-theorist, dude-bro son would love; that my athletic, competitive, bulked-up son would love; and that my uber-sensitive, literal, hamburger-hating baby would love. (Related: This family is all over the place. We spend a lot of money on therapy.)

<u>Stone-cold fact: Every weirdo in my family loves this burger.</u> Not because it's healthy or vegan or good for the earth. Because it is DELICIOUS. Huge flavor, perfect texture, entirely satisfying. You are making this. I am not messing around with you.

2 medium sweet potatoes

—

½ cup uncooked quinoa (whatever, man)

—

1 (15-ounce) can black beans, drained and rinsed

1½ cups quick-cooking oats

1 small or ½ large red onion, chopped

1 bunch cilantro, chopped

3 garlic cloves, minced

1 tablespoon ground cumin

1 tablespoon chili powder

2 tablespoons adobo sauce (from a can of chipotle peppers in adobo)

Salt and black pepper

—

Oil, for brushing

FOR SERVING (PICK WHATEVER YOU LIKE)

Trash Sauce (page 103), tons of it

Chipotle mayo (dice 2 chipotle peppers from the can you just opened and mix with ⅓ cup mayo)

Hamburger buns (Hawaiian buns are too delicious and cannot be bested here)

Beautiful ripe tomato slices

Sliced avocado

Thinly sliced onion

Butter lettuce leaves

If you're absolutely going for it: 1 over-medium egg per burger

// Let's get those sweet potatoes going. Preheat your oven to 400°F. Throw the sweet potatoes on a foil-lined baking sheet and roast for 30 to 40 minutes, until they are fork-tender. Remove them from the oven and let cool until they won't burn your fingers off, then peel. The skin comes right off, so this is easier than it sounds. (You can either griddle or bake these burgers, so leave the oven on if you're going with the latter.)

// Meanwhile, cook the quinoa according to the package directions and set aside.

// In a large bowl, combine the peeled sweet potatoes, cooked quinoa, and everything from "black beans to salt and black pepper." Grab your potato masher (or hand mixer!) and mash and mash until this becomes burger mush. Don't be judgmental—raw ground beef is also burger mush, and way grosser at that, so that is just how this is. Vegetarian burgers have rights too.

RECIPE CONTINUES

// Form the burger mush into thin patties (for more sear and less mush) and stick them in the fridge for 20 minutes to firm up.

// My favorite way to cook these is on a hot griddle, because I love the sear, but get excited, because you can also bake these for a no-mess, no-fuss option; just brush them generously with oil and throw them into your oven (still at 400°F) for about 30 minutes, flipping them once halfway through. Otherwise, fire up your griddle on medium-high heat, brush each burger liberally with oil, and cook those babies for about 8 minutes per side, until seared and golden.

// Meanwhile, throw together your Trash Sauce (if using) and set aside. Or your chipotle mayo. Or both! What a wonderful world! Slice and dice your burger toppings. If you're over-medium-egging it, start firing those up while the burgers are cooking.

// I'm not kidding here. These are so yummy, and not just as some dumb vegetarian substitute for better food. I make these ON PURPOSE because the end result is so phenomenal. They are hearty (and healthy) and jam-packed with flavor, and your carnivores will gobble these up like unsuspecting little vegan piggies.

Note

These freeze beautifully. Double the recipe, patty them up, and store half in your freezer.

MUJADARA with ZHOUG

My two youngest kids are from Ethiopia, which introduced me to lentils, which introduced me to mujadara, which introduced me to zhoug, which ended up in this cookbook, which ended up in your Amazon cart, which ended up in your hands. And now you have Ben and Remy Hatmaker to thank for the utterly delicious layered dish you're about to make.

I'm going to say this right up front: don't bother making this if you aren't willing to include every single layer. If you're turning up your nose at the caramelized onions because they take too long or the zhoug because you don't know what it is (it's like a Middle Eastern chimichurri), just turn to another page and make Chicken Potpie (that's page 141). Individually, these layers are fine. (I mean, what do you want me to say about rice?) But all together, and I mean ALL TOGETHER, this dish creates the perfect bite. I fed this to my brother recently, and he asked, "Where is the protein?" and I was like, "Do you not see those lentils?" and he was like, "Why does God hate me?" and then he ate three bowls. You can't argue with the perfect bite.

Don't feel weird about this long list of ingredients. Most of them are in your spice cabinet.

SWAP
roasted butternut squash for the sweet potatoes.

ZHOUG

4 garlic cloves

2 cups fresh cilantro

1 jalapeño, seeded

½ teaspoon salt

½ teaspoon ground cardamom

½ teaspoon ground cumin

½ teaspoon red pepper flakes

Juice of 1 lemon

¾ to 1 cup extra-virgin olive oil

CARAMELIZED ONIONS

4 large onions, sliced

2 tablespoons extra-virgin olive oil

2 tablespoons butter

Salt and pepper

RICE AND LENTILS

4 garlic cloves, chopped

2 tablespoons ground cumin

2 tablespoons smoked paprika

2 teaspoons onion powder

2 teaspoons salt

2 teaspoons cayenne pepper

1 teaspoon black pepper

2 bay leaves

8 cups veggie stock

2 cups uncooked brown basmati rice

16 ounces dried brown lentils, rinsed and drained

—

4 sweet potatoes, peeled and diced

Olive oil

Salt and pepper

—

Plain Greek yogurt, for serving

// Let's start with the zhoug, because it gets better as it sits in the fridge. Here are the very complicated instructions for making it: Put everything on the zhoug list into your blender or food processor and blend. The end. This spicy, herby sauce is my boyfriend. Want to be your own hero? Make this the day before, stick it in the fridge, and cross it off the list.

RECIPE CONTINUES

// Then let's get those onions going, because these go low and slow like risotto, and though you know they'll grow dynamo, a fast flow is a no-go. (It took me 15 minutes to invent that rhyme and it doesn't even make sense. Idc, it stands.) Throw all those onions, the oil, butter, and some salt and pepper into a large skillet and let the onions cook over medium-low heat until Jesus comes back, stirring occasionally. These can go for 45 minutes or whatever. Until they're just the most delicious sweet brown things you've ever seen. This is a good time to start preheating your oven to 400°F for the sweet potatoes.

// While the onions are cooking down, you're going to cook the rice and lentils together in one pot; it's a wonderful time to be alive when this can happen. In a stockpot or Dutch oven, combine the ingredients from "garlic through veggie stock" and bring to a boil over medium-high heat. Add the rice and lentils and stir to combine. Lower the heat, put a lid on it, and cook for 30 minutes, until the lentils are tender. Remove the bay leaves before serving.

// **I've added a** nontraditional final layer **with the sweet potatoes, so my apologies to the Middle Eastern grandmas.** Toss your sweet potatoes on a baking sheet with olive oil, salt, and pepper and roast for 20 minutes, until they are tender and browning on the edges. (Buy cubed peeled sweet potato in the produce section if you want to live your best life.)

// GET EXCITED, EVERYONE.

// Grab a big beautiful platter to serve this family-style. Layer it all up: rice and lentils, caramelized onions, then roasted sweet potatoes. *Liberally* drizzle the zhoug all over and dollop on the yogurt. I'm serious: do not be stingy with the sauce and yogurt, because they WAKE UP those other layers. Every single thing needs to be in every single bite. The worst thing about this dish is that it dirties up a ton of dishes. The best thing about it is everything else. "Where is the protein," my ass.

Notes

OTHER THINGS TO PUT ZHOUG ON

eggs, salads, sandwiches, tacos, hummus, roasted veggies, beans

MARGHERITA Pizza

WITH Pesto and House Sauce

Most home cooks have a signature move: mine is homemade pizza. If I had to choose one thing to eat for the rest of my life, it would be a dead tie between pizza and sandwiches. (A discerning reader will notice an entire chapter called "Food That Goes in Carbs," so devoted am I to the sandwich. You may be asking, "I'm curious how someone whose favorite food is a sandwich gets to write a cookbook?" I blame the patriarchy!)

But right now this is about homemade pizza, not the pedestrian sandwich. Once you make this three or four times and get past the "rules" of it, you'll no longer need a recipe and this will go into your weekly rotation. It has a 100% success, approval, and satisfaction rate. **It is so worth it to make your own dough, and so easy even a caveman can do it in his stand mixer.**

Outside of a few fresh ingredients, you probably have everything you need for homemade pizza. Let's go.

DOUGH

1 teaspoon active dry yeast (about half a ¼-ounce packet)

1½ cups warm water

1 teaspoon sugar

—

4 cups flour

1 teaspoon sea salt

⅓ cup olive oil

1 teaspoon Italian seasoning (optional)

1 tablespoon honey (optional)

FOR TOPPING

House Sauce (page 104)

1 (7-ounce) container pesto

2 ripe, beautiful tomatoes (if you can buy these from a farmer, gold star for you), thinly sliced

Leaves from 1 bunch basil, torn or sliced

16 ounces fresh mozzarella cheese

Red pepper flakes (optional)

Balsamic Reduction (page 103), for drizzling (optional)

// Get things started 2 to 3 hours in advance: Sprinkle the yeast over the warm water and then stir in the sugar. Let it proof and bubble while you do the rest.

// In the bowl of your stand mixer (or in a large bowl), mix the flour and salt on low speed. With the mixer running, drizzle in the olive oil and mix until incorporated, then drizzle in the yeast mixture. If you like just a bare touch of savory and sweet, add the Italian seasoning and honey. Let your mixer knead the dough for 4 to 5 minutes on medium speed, or knead it by hand. (The fatal dough flaw: undermixing. If you knead it long enough, it will become pliable and smooth. Not enough, and it is sticky and crumbly.)

// Drizzle a bit of olive oil into a clean bowl, put the ball of dough in the bowl, and turn it to coat it with oil all around. Cover the bowl with a damp towel and let the dough rise for 2 to 3 hours, until doubled in size.

// This whole thing takes 10 minutes (rising time excluded). Why does dough seem fancy??

// One hour before pizza time, start your House Sauce. That recipe makes twice as much as you need just so you could use half today and pop the other half in your freezer for next time.

// Preheat your oven as hot as it will go (around the 500°F mark). I bake my pizzas on a cast-iron pizza pan, but you can use a baking sheet. Throw it in the oven to get hot while you get the pizza ready.

// Divide your risen dough into fourths, wrap two portions individually in plastic wrap, and stick those in your freezer too. Now you have dough and sauce for your next pizza night, and as you're enjoying that low-prep meal, you will fill your mind with the fondest thoughts of me. I accept this honor.

// Assuming you put half the dough in the freezer, you'll be left with enough dough to make two pizzas, which you will bake one at a time. (Want four pizzas right now? Make four right now. This is the Land of the Free and the Home of the Brave.)

// Flour your counter and roll out one portion of the dough. I like a thin, crispy crust, but you could roll yours out thicker, all soft and squishy, if you're not spiritually mature in the area of crusts.

RECIPE CONTINUES

// Once your oven and pizza pan are scorching hot, drizzle some olive oil on the pan and arrange your dough on top. The edges of your crust can be a hot mess. I just bend and fold mine all into place. Pop it in the oven for around 4 minutes, then carefully take it out (a 500°F pan is no joke, says the nice lady who has a few burn scars from this step) and ladle on your sauce. Spread a layer of pesto over the sauce with the back of a spoon, then add your toppings, as much or as little as you want. It's pizza! And you are the boss of it!

// Back into the oven for another 5 to 6 minutes, until everything is melted perfection and your crust looks nice and toasty. Let it cool for a couple of minutes before slicing it up and becoming the Family Hero. My first pizza is always completely gone before I even get the second one in the oven.

// I know this seems like a lot of steps, but they are parceled out over an afternoon. You just knock it out 10 minutes at a time in between other stuff. Plus, don't forget that every other time, YOU'LL HAVE READY-MADE DOUGH AND SAUCE. Welcome to your life of leisure.

> ## Note
>
> This is so fun to make as individual grilled pizzas: Set up a toppings bar so everyone can do their own. Roll out personal-size crusts, grill on one side until toasted, then remove from the heat and add sauce and toppings to the grilled side. Return the pizzas to the grill to finish cooking. The grill master has to be ON TOP OF THIS, but it's the perfect party food.

VEGGIE, PESTO, AND CHEESE

STUFFED SHELLS

SAUCE

3 tablespoons olive oil

4 garlic cloves, chopped

1½ teaspoons red pepper flakes

1 (24-ounce) jar of your favorite marinara sauce

1 tablespoon sugar

Salt and black pepper

—

1 (12-ounce) box jumbo pasta shells

—

2 tablespoons olive oil

1 (8-ounce) container cremini mushrooms, very finely diced

½ cup dry white wine

1 tablespoon Italian seasoning

5 ounces baby spinach

2 cups whole-milk ricotta cheese

1 (7-ounce) container pesto

2 cups grated Parmesan cheese (8 ounces)

3 tablespoons chopped fresh oregano

Growing up, Mom cooked our favorite dish on our birthdays. I have no idea what my sibs chose because I am the oldest and thus the center of my childhood universe, but I never varied one time from my request: manicotti. I had it every year that my mom gave a damn, which was probably 65% (you can't care about every birthday when you have four kids).

Stuffed cheesy saucy pasta is why God invented Italy. No need for meat. All we need here is cheese and sauce and some other filler designed to soak up those flavors and deliver them to our mouths. As an adult cook, I transitioned to large pasta shells from manicotti for one reason only: they are easier. Now you know how I operate as a grown-up.

This recipe is a hybrid between "Food for Hippies" and "No More Damns to Give," because I am offering you jarred marinara and pesto, and it comes together in a New York minute. If you think your children won't eat this because of the mushrooms, think again, sport, because they won't even know. Now that I think of it, this is also a hybrid with "Food for Your Picky Spouse or Spawn" because we are tricking them.

God, this is so good.

NOTE If you're interested in three cheeses, top this with fresh mozzarella before baking. We do what we want.

// Preheat your oven to 400°F.

// Let's get that sauce going. In a saucepan, combine the oil, garlic, and red pepper flakes and cook over medium heat for 3 minutes, until the garlic is fragrant but not browned. Add the marinara, sugar, and salt and black pepper to taste and whisk until combined. Lower the heat and simmer for at least 30 minutes. (If you have House Sauce in the freezer like I've instructed, sub that right in here; you'll need 3 cups.)

// Meanwhile, bring a pot of salted water to a boil, add the pasta shells, and cook until still veeeeeery al dente, 8 to 9 minutes. Drain immediately and rinse under cold water.

// Also meanwhile, in a skillet, heat the olive oil over medium-high heat. Add the mushrooms and cook until they have released their liquid and browned up beautifully, 5 minutes or so. Then add the wine and Italian seasoning, season with salt and pepper, and cook until the liquid has reduced by half, another 3 minutes or so. Add the spinach and toss until it is totally wilted, 2 to 3 minutes. Transfer this whole delicious mixture to a bowl.

// To that mushroomy, spinachy mix, add the ricotta, pesto, 1 cup of the Parm, and the oregano and stir until totally combined.

// **Build time:** Spoon 1 cup of the marinara into a 9 x 13-inch baking dish and swirl to coat the bottom of the dish. Nestle the pasta shells on top of the sauce. Spoon a dollop of the cheesy-pesto-mushroom mix into each shell, filling them to capacity but not to overflowing. Pour the remaining marinara over the stuffed shells and top with the remaining 1 cup Parmesan.

// Bake until golden and bubbling, around 20 minutes. Serve this with garlic bread and who cares what else. This is all that matters.

FOOD *FOR* WHEN YOU HAVE NO MORE DAMNS *TO* GIVE

7

SHORTCUTS, SEMI-HOMEMADE MEALS & LEFTOVERS

GREEN CHILE TACO CUPS

1 pound lean ground beef

1 (1-ounce) packet taco seasoning (Do I buy the "hot" version? You know I do.)

1 (14.5-ounce) can petite diced tomatoes, drained (or just dice up 2 tomatoes if you have them)

1 (4-ounce) can diced green chiles

—

Nonstick cooking spray

1 (16-ounce) package square wonton wrappers, thawed if frozen

2 cups shredded sharp cheddar cheese (8 ounces)

Oil, for brushing

FOR SERVING

Shredded iceberg lettuce

Sour cream

Salsa

Diced scallions or chopped cilantro (or both!)

Kids are so predictable, man. All you have to do is run a few trick plays and you can get them to gobble up new food. They don't even know that you are sneaking in ground cauliflower or whatever. Pour it into a fun shape, or sandwich it between tortillas, or serve it in individual ramekins, or blend it into oblivion. Look, provide a side sauce for dipping? They'll eat raw habaneros.

But even if they're already adventurous eaters, everyone—including you—will love these green chile taco cups. They are adorable. They are delicious. They are basically tacos, so let's not overreact (everyone knows tacos are a "No Damns" dinner choice), but the presentation is super fun. Serve these with Green Chile Chorizo Queso (page 61), and you've created a bona fide Mexican spread. (And if your kids don't like Mexican food, consider upgrading.)

These are on the table in 30 minutes, and the hardest step is browning ground beef.

SWAP
ground turkey for the ground beef.

// Preheat your oven to 375°F.

// Fire up a skillet over medium heat. Brown the ground beef until it is no longer pink, 6 to 8 minutes, then drain off any fat. Back on the burner, add the taco seasoning, tomatoes, and green chiles to the beef and stir until combined. Add a little bit of water and stir until it all comes together. Take the pan off the heat.

// Now, wonton wrappers + muffin tins are a revelation. You're basically making tiny individual taco bowls, and if that isn't the cutest thing you've ever heard of, I must be explaining cuteness wrong. Spray a muffin tin with nonstick spray and line each cup with one wonton wrapper. Just press it in there and let the edges fold up the sides. Throw these in the oven as is for 5 minutes to set them, then let cool for a couple of minutes.

// Fill each wonton cup with 1 tablespoon of the meat, followed by a sprinkling of cheese. Then layer each cup with one more wonton wrapper and press down, letting the edges fold over the sides. Add another tablespoon of meat and top with cheese. Brush the edges of the wonton wrapper with a little oil. A double taco cup! The cuteness hurts my eyes!

// Pop these babies into the oven for about 10 minutes, until the cheese has melted and the edges of the wonton wrappers are browned and crunchy. Then the trick is this: Let them cool in the muffin tin for at least 5 minutes before removing them from the pan (if you can squeeze out 10 minutes, they will hold their shape best, but starving children are maniacs, so just do your best).

// **Set up your taco cup bar:** shredded iceberg, sour cream, salsa, and scallions or cilantro. Everyone gets their own little baby taco cup(s), and you are a hero. My 6-foot-tall grown children are like, "Mom! Yummy! So cute!" I rest my case.

Red Curry with Whatever You Have

I didn't have a solitary bite of Thai food until my thirties, and thus I want to retroactively take my parents to small claims court: "Your honor, Larry and Jana King defined 'exotic cuisine' as 'food from California,' and I'd like to petition for reparations for neglect. I'd also like to be compensated ex post facto for eating nothing but oat bran from 1988 to 1991 because my dad was doing Bill Phillips's 'Body for Life.' We suffered, Judge."

Turns out, Thai food is my favorite in all the lands. It is the cuisine I always choose when my friends force me to play horrible games like "If you could only eat food from one country for the rest of your life" and "If you had to pick your least favorite kid . . ." (Don't be silly. They were all my least favorite between roughly sixth and eighth grade. Every one of those clowns has been on the D list.)

Sweet, spicy, creamy, salty, crunchy . . . I want to marry Thai food and have all its babies. On nights when you have no time and no damns, I give you red curry, because it is as easy as spaghetti but ten million times more delicious. Well, easy the way I make it, which is the way you are going to make it, because you paid for this cookbook and now you have to do what I say. You need two main ingredients that you might not have on hand: curry paste (see Note on page 186) and canned coconut milk (do not get low-fat or whatever satanic version).

Besides the curry paste and coconut milk (and rice!), you literally have everything else, because curry is whatever you have. Start your rice first, because the rest comes together so fast, you'll still be waiting on it. **(My rice cooker is my live-in boyfriend. We have a beautiful relationship. He has never failed me. I would save him from a house fire.)**

Now, look in your veggie drawer. Look in your potato and onion bin. What is on its last leg? That is going in your curry. There is no possible wrong combination. Only have one vegetable? That's now your play: "Family, we are having chicken and half-an-onion curry." (The last time I made this, I used purple onion, bulb onions, and red bell peppers that were WRINKLED.) Anything goes: broccoli, cauliflower, potatoes, snap peas, peppers, baby corn like Tom Hanks ate in *Big*, carrots, asparagus, squash, I don't even care.

Same goes for your protein, if you even want one: chicken, beef, shrimp, sausage, tofu, paneer cheese. Or leftover meat, which you'll just slice and throw in at the very end to warm through. Whatever you have is what you're putting in your curry. See how flexible this is? No one tells you those rubbery carrots are too far gone.

RECIPE CONTINUES

2 tablespoons olive oil

3 to 4 cups thinly sliced
veggies (any) and protein
(or none)

Salt and pepper

—

2 to 3 tablespoons red
curry paste (or green
curry paste, if you prefer!)

2 (13.5-ounce) cans full-fat
coconut milk

—

White or jasmine rice,
cooked according to the
package directions

Chopped fresh parsley
or basil, for serving
(optional)

> ## Note
>
> You can get red curry paste ON THE
> INTERNET because Jesus loves us.
> My fave brand is Mae Ploy; it lives on
> Amazon, just waiting to be on your
> doorstep tomorrow.

// Heat the olive oil in a skillet over medium-high heat. Add your veggies and some salt and pepper and sauté for about 5 minutes. If you're using a super-sturdy vegetable like cauliflower or butternut squash, this may take a little longer; sauté until they are tender.

// Add 2 tablespoons of the curry paste and stir to incorporate. Home chef, some of this stuff is spicy. You can always add more, but you cannot undo the fire. I always overdo this by about double. I wish I was sorry, but I'm not. Drink more water, kids. Add the coconut milk and whisk until smooth. Look at that creamy sauce you just made out of two cans and some store-bought paste. Taste this and see if you like it. Might need to add a bit more curry paste or salt (and a splash of fish sauce, if you have it, but don't tell your children because they are THE WORST about fish sauce, except when it makes their food delicious and they don't know).

// Add your protein and poach until cooked through (the timing will vary depending on what you're using). Or just have veggie curry and let a chicken live to see another day.

// All this takes 12 minutes. Your rice isn't even done.

// Spoon this awesomeness over the rice. Scatter it with parsley or basil if you have some that's about to become a health hazard in your veggie drawer. The amount that I love curry is ten million.

PASTA BAKE

WITH *House Cream Sauce*

I would be embarrassed to include this recipe, except this chapter is called "Food for When You Have No More Damns to Give," and I'm assuming that's where you find yourself at this juncture. This is a lazy lasagna, so welcome to my food POV. It is so dumb because your family will love this. It's no fail and also no damns, so you're welcome for this fancy cookbook.

House Sauce is my staple red sauce, and I make it around the clock like a little old Italian grandma. My thesis is this: you will make the House Sauce, you will triple the quantities, you will portion and freeze it, and thus you will always have some ready to go. If not, it comes together in 5 minutes, then just needs to simmer for an hour. MAKE TRIPLE. SAVE YOURSELF.

Nonstick cooking spray

1 (16-ounce) package
fettuccine

—

1 small onion, diced

4 garlic cloves, diced

1 pound ground Italian
sausage (sweet, hot,
whatever)

Salt and pepper

—

6 cups House Sauce
(page 104)

1 cup heavy cream

—

1 (15-ounce) container
whole-milk ricotta cheese

1 pound fresh mozzarella
(in a log or ball)

¾ cup grated Parmesan
cheese (3 ounces)

3 tablespoons Italian
seasoning

3 tablespoons chopped
fresh basil or parsley

// Preheat your oven to 400°F and spray a 9 x 13-inch baking dish with nonstick spray.

// If you're making the House Sauce now, start that first so it has time to simmer. If you made some in advance, heat it over low heat while you do the rest.

// Cook the fettuccine according to the package directions. I like a long noodle for this bake because it acts like a layer barrier, more like a lasagna noodle but without the annoying step of shoving lasagna planks into a pot to boil. I've used fusilli and elbow macaroni, but all the stuff melts through those shapes, making it indecipherable pasta mush. Does it still taste good? Of course it does! Look at this ingredient list!

// While the noodles are boiling, combine the onion, garlic, and sausage with some salt and pepper in a skillet and cook over medium heat until the sausage is browned.

// Stir the cream into your warm House Sauce. Oooohhhh myyyy goooosh.

// Drain the pasta, then grab that baking dish—

IT'S LAYER TIME

+ One-third of the House (Cream) Sauce.
+ One third of the cooked fettuccine.
+ One third of the sausage mix.
+ One third of the ricotta, dolloped straight out of the container.
+ One third of the mozzarella, straight out of the package (if you bought the presliced kind; otherwise, slice it first).
+ One layer of sprinkled Parmesan. Straight out of the bag.
+ A tablespoon of Italian seasoning.
+ Repeat two more times, ending with Parm on top.

// Cover with foil and bake for 45 minutes. Take the foil off and bake for 5 minutes more, or until the cheese is browning and everything is bubbling and you literally cannot handle the goodness. Sprinkle with the basil or parsley.

// This is the meanest thing I have ever said, but let it rest, uncovered, for 10 minutes. Let it settle and firm up and lower itself from the temperature of the sun. Eat this with chunks of buttered garlic bread to sop up the sauce and cheese. I don't even care if we have a vegetable. Basil is a plant.

Pasta Bake
with House
Cream Sauce
187

PORK OR CHICKEN OR BEEF OR SHRIMP

Fried Rice

4 tablespoons neutral oil (canola, grapeseed, whatever)

3 tablespoons butter

1 small onion, chopped

½ cup small-diced carrots (my fave is using bagged shredded carrots)

1 cup frozen peas

3 garlic cloves, minced

2 tablespoons minced fresh ginger

3 to 4 cups leftover rice

2 large eggs, beaten

1 cup or so cubed or shredded leftover cooked meat (or none! We aren't cooking new meat for this, people.)

¼ cup soy sauce

1½ teaspoons toasted sesame oil

1½ teaspoons fish sauce

Salt and pepper

Chopped scallions, for serving

Sriracha, for drizzling (optional)

This recipe is so low on damns, it doesn't actually make sense for how delicious it is. I don't even know if this counts as a recipe, but my brother insisted I include it, because I make this all the time and he loves it, and I do what he wants because that is the rule in our family.

Sidebar: Moms of a bunch of girls and one boy, particularly if he is the baby? Don't worry if the girls torture that little dumplin' right now. Never mind if they dress him up or paint his nails or tell him lies about who his parents are. He will grow up and be the Reigning Prince of the Siblings, and he will get what he wants and they will all kowtow to his preferences. He will get the last laugh while also being incredibly well versed in melodrama, girl fights, and tampons.

I am counting on you having two leftovers on hand here: rice and meat, any meat. So plan on cooking this during a week when you're making rice for something else, and make sure you have leftovers. Fried rice actually only works with day-old rice straight out of the fridge. The meat is anything you have in a container. My friend Jeff even uses brisket in his fried rice, so you do you, boo. This is leftover food repurposed, so look in your Tupperwares to see where your food journey is going to take you.

The hardest thing you're going to do here is chop the garlic and ginger and scallions. Grab a large wok or the biggest skillet you have and a couple of wooden spatulas. There are three parts to fried rice: frying the veggies, frying the rice, and scrambling the eggs. Honestly? This can reasonably go in any order, but this is how I like it best for sure.

// Heat your skillet over high heat until it is nice and hot. Add 2 tablespoons each of the oil and butter, then immediately throw in the onion and carrots. Sauté until the veggies are just starting to soften, 3 to 4 minutes. Add the peas, garlic, and ginger and stir another minute. Transfer all the veggies to a bowl with a slotted spoon, leaving the oil and butter in the pan. (I don't like the veggies overcooked or the rice undercooked, and this is my solution.)

// Add the remaining 1 tablespoon butter and 2 tablespoons oil to the hot skillet, then dump in the cold rice, breaking up any clumps. Basically you want each grain of rice coated in the buttery oil first, so use your two spatulas to toss and toss. Let it sit, unstirred, on the hot skillet bottom for a minute at a time to really brown, then toss and repeat. Do this for anywhere from 5 to 8 minutes, until the rice is FRIED. I am uninterested in warmed rice. I want it fried, dammit.

// Make a well in the center of the skillet and pour in the beaten eggs. Quick-scramble them with your spatula. Return the veggies to the pan and add whatever meat you're using (if you're using any). In a small bowl, whisk together the soy sauce, sesame oil, and fish sauce and pour over the entire skillet. Add salt and pepper and toss until absolutely everything is combined. Give a quick taste to see if it needs anything else. Take it off the heat and sprinkle with chopped scallions.

// This all takes about 15 minutes, and it is heaven in a bowl, as good as any restaurant's. We drizzle our fried rice with sriracha, of course, because the only thing better than flavor is more flavor. I have never, not one time, been able to eat only one bowl. The Reigning Prince of the Siblings eats three.

Taco Soup

1 tablespoon oil

1 pound 85% lean ground beef

1 onion, chopped

1 or 2 jalapeños, diced

4 garlic cloves, chopped

___

2 (14-ounce) cans diced tomatoes, with their juices

1 (14-ounce) can black beans, drained and rinsed

1 (14-ounce) can pinto beans, drained and rinsed

1 (14-ounce) can shoepeg (or white) corn, drained

2 (4-ounce) cans diced green chiles

1 (28-ounce) can crushed tomatoes

2 (1-ounce) packets taco seasoning

2 (1-ounce) packets ranch seasoning mix

Salt and pepper

FOR TOPPING (ANY OR ALL)

Sour cream

Shredded cheddar

Chopped cilantro

Diced avocados

Diced red onion

Pickled jalapeños

Corn chips or tortilla chips (my dad likes saltine crackers)

Can you open a bunch of canned goods? Then congratulations: You have the skill set for this recipe. This is chili's second cousin, but dumber. Like every recipe in this section, the ROI is way too high for the investment. This is for:

1. Feeding a ton of people.
2. Needing super good food with a low risk factor for screwing it up.
3. Wanting to spend almost zero energy.
4. Those of you invested in the canned goods stock market.

I love this on game day because it can sit on a warm burner all the livelong day and people can eat when they damn well feel like it. The toppings bar stays out, the lid stays on, and you don't have to post up in the kitchen while everyone else is having fun. You can make an absolute trough of taco soup, because it is even better the next day. I once ate the leftovers for eight straight days and never got tired of it. Related: I am not precious about food expiration AT ALL. My butter lives on the counter, I'll eat anything past its prime, and I make fried rice out of week-old rice. **America needs to calm down.**

// You look me in the face and tell me this recipe isn't absurd. PEEP THAT LIST OF CANNED GOODS. Do not let your friends see your recycling bin when they come over for this. The jig will officially be up. This is so dumb, but I am telling you, it tastes so good. No damns to be found here.

// **This is the very hardest part:** In a Dutch oven, heat the oil over medium heat, then add the ground beef, onion, and jalapeños and cook until the meat is no longer pink, around 8 minutes. Drain any rendered fat, then add the garlic and cook for another minute or two. This concludes the labor portion of this recipe, except for the carpal tunnel you are about to experience with the cans.

// Into the Dutch oven, add everything else on the list except the toppings ("diced tomatoes through salt and pepper"). LOL! What are we doing here?? If the soup feels too thick, add some water. Let this come to a boil, then lower the heat and simmer for around 20 minutes to let the flavors meld. Give it a little taste and see if it needs more salt. Want more spice? Add some cayenne. Is it a little flat? Squeeze in some lime juice.

// Lower the heat and just leave it on your stove for the people to self-serve. Set up your scrumptious toppings bar. It is now every man for himself. I have never met a single person who doesn't adore taco soup. Shelf-stable canned goods have redeemed themselves from their '80s PR nightmare.

Fajitas al Guajillo

Yes, this is a No Damns recipe because everyone knows fajitas are a Level 1 endeavor, and we are doing this all in one skillet, but first let me tell you about Polvos. In the weirdest little section of South First Street is a divey restaurant with a tragic parking lot and a whacked-out paint job. There isn't a single local Austinite who doesn't love Polvos, which specializes in interior Mexican food. I drive visiting guests straight there so they can immediately start living. You watch the cooks make homemade tortillas while you load up at the salsa bar, and if that sentence doesn't explain it, then I can't help here.

This is no exaggeration. the first time I ever went to Polvos, over twenty years ago, I ordered fajitas al guajillo. I have easily been there fifty times since, and I have never ordered anything else. Not once. I can't bring myself to not have them. I'm sure the rest of the menu is equally fantastic, but I'll never know.

This is my home version, which will never, ever be as good as the original, but since you don't live in Austin, this is what you're stuck with. Yes, I know there is some nontraditional fajita stuff here, but you're going to have to trust Polvos and Jen Hatmaker, who has ordered this dish fifty straight times.

MARINADE

3 or 4 canned chipotle peppers in adobo sauce

4 garlic cloves

¾ cup olive oil

Juice of 2 limes

2 teaspoons ground cumin

Salt and black pepper

—

4 or 5 boneless, skinless chicken thighs

Corn or flour tortillas

—

2 tablespoons high-temp oil (grapeseed, canola, whatever)

1 large onion, sliced

1 poblano pepper, seeded and sliced

—

¼ cup golden raisins

¼ cup pecan halves

¼ cup peanuts

FOR SERVING

Shredded Monterey Jack cheese

Sour cream

// You are going to give an early damn for this scrumptious recipe so you'll have to give almost none come dinnertime. Either the night before or the morning of, before your day goes into the gutter, let's get that chicken flavored up. Marinade time: Combine the chipotles, garlic, olive oil, lime juice, cumin, and a little salt and black pepper in your blender and zip it up. I'd start with 3 chipotles, then have a taste. These smoky gems are the secret to this marinade, but they can be spicy. You can always add a fourth, but you can't put feeling back into your mouth.

// Slice your chicken into strips and stick it in a large zip-top bag. Raw chicken is the worst and I hate it. I wish there was another way. I know I'm being fussy, but I said what I said. Pour the marinade over the chicken, seal the baggie, and stick it in the fridge for the rest of the day or overnight. Now that's ready for later. Your fajita chicken is already sliced, for crying out loud. You're practically feeding your people with a baby spoon.

GOES GREAT WITH

an ice-cold Mexican beer with lime.

RECIPE CONTINUES

// When it's time to cook, preheat your oven to 350°F, wrap your tortillas in foil, and throw them in there to warm through. (Using corn tortillas? I always toast them on each side over my gas burner, holding them with tongs, because I like a little char on those bad boys. You could also toast these up on a griddle.)

// In a large skillet, heat the oil over medium-high heat. Add the chicken strips and sauté until cooked through, 6 to 8 minutes or so. Because you did the pre-work by slicing it, it will cook fast. Cut into the fattest piece to make sure there is no pink in the middle.

// With tongs, transfer the chicken to a plate. With all that leftover marinade and chicken juice and oil still over medium-high heat, add the sliced onion and poblano. I like my fajitas veggies absolutely caramelized, so let these sit on that hot skillet to BROWN UP for 8 to 10 minutes.

// Finally, when your veggies are the color you like, add the raisins, pecans, and peanuts and sauté for about 3 minutes. Return the chicken to the pan and totally combine it all like a big sizzling skillet of fajitas you get at Polvos.

// Proper Mexican food eating means corn tortillas, but something went dreadfully wrong in my house, and I am THE ONLY PERSON who loves corn tortillas. My children were all raised in Austin, so I don't know what the hell happened here. My dum-dums tuck all this into flour tortillas. Whatever you choose, don't skip the Monterey Jack cheese or the sour cream. **You may now apologize for whatever bad thoughts you had when you saw the raisins and pecans and peanuts in the ingredient list.** This is utter magic. If Polvos ever rotates fajitas al guajillo off their menu, I will riot up in these streets.

Note

You can also marinate the chicken whole, throw it on the grill, and slice it after cooking.

Risotto WITH Whatever You Have

I didn't grow up eating risotto because I guess it didn't exist in the United States in the '80s. Or maybe it showed up in New York City and LA, but definitely not in Middle America. It skipped us, much like kale and diversity. But then I grew up and ate risotto for the first time at a dinner party, and I was *besotted. What is this?? Rice? Soup rice? Sauce rice? Creamed rice?* I started asking around in my new Risotto Vision Quest, and people acted really melodramatic: "It is SO much work." "You are STUCK at the stove." "I only make this if I'm trying to procure a PROPOSAL."

Turns out, they were just being histrionic, an emotional ploy I've never partaken in, obviously. So before we get to the recipe, let me give you the primary rules of risotto:

1. Put on your favorite show. I like something soothing like a British crime drama starring Olivia Colman. Make anyone who says British shows are "boring" with "not enough action" leave the room. This is your time. This is your kingdom.

2. Pour a cold glass of the delicious white wine you will be using for this recipe into your favorite goblet.

3. Put that wine in your nondominant hand.

4. Hold and enjoy your wine for the 20 minutes your dominant hand is adding warm stock and stirring your risotto to creamy perfection.

5. Consider adding more butter and Parmesan than your recipe calls for, even this one by your beloved Jen. And of course way more cracked black pepper. Have you ever thought, "This has too much butter and cheese in it"? No, you haven't. Don't get weird.

Basically risotto is a dreamy way to stand in your kitchen, drink your wine, watch your show, stir your rice, and delight every member of your family with creamy, buttery, cheesy happiness. You can even get them to eat peas, because that is the power of risotto. Outside of the basic risotto staples in the main recipe, whatever you have is what goes in.

Before we get to it, look around your kitchen to see what you have to add to this. To be absolutely sure, you can make it exactly as written and live happily ever after. This is the basic risotto operation, and it is divine. But you can elevate this at the end with whatever is in your fridge (peep your leftover containers!) or pantry, like:

+ **1 cup frozen peas, stirred in at the end**
+ **1 (8-ounce) container any kind of mushrooms, diced and sautéed separately**
+ **1 (12-ounce) jar roasted red peppers, drained and sliced**
+ **1 cup cubed roasted butternut squash**
+ **½ cup sun-dried tomatoes, whole or chopped**
+ **1 bunch asparagus, sliced and sautéed**
+ **Several dollops of pesto**
+ **1 (15-ounce) can creamy white beans, drained, rinsed, and added during the last 10 minutes**
+ **2 cups ground hot Italian sausage, browned, drained, and added at the end**
+ **A fried egg to top each serving**
+ **Roasted shrimp**
+ **Leftover cooked meat: shredded chicken, diced pork tenderloin, thinly sliced steak, chopped ham, whatever**
+ **If you are absolutely GOING FOR IT: big gorgeous lobster chunks. I die.**

RECIPE CONTINUES

6 cups chicken stock (veggie stock would work too!)

—

1 tablespoon olive oil

4 tablespoons (½ stick) butter

1 large shallot, or ½ small onion, chopped

2 cups uncooked Arborio rice

½ cup dry white wine (don't forget rules #2 through #4 on the previous page)

—

½ cup grated Parmesan cheese (2 ounces)

3 tablespoons chopped fresh chives, or ½ cup chopped fresh parsley

1 teaspoon salt

Pleeeeeeeenty of cracked pepper

NOTE
WHAT TO DO WITH LEFTOVER RISOTTO

Turn it into magical fried galettes the next morning. Simply form it into patties (it will firm way up in the fridge overnight), dredge in a little flour, and fry in a few tablespoons of olive oil over medium–high heat, about 4 minutes per side.

// Pour your stock into a saucepan over low heat and keep it at a simmer.

// Heat the olive oil and 2 tablespoons of the butter in a large skillet or Dutch oven over medium heat, then add the shallot and cook, stirring, for 2 minutes. Add the rice and cook, stirring, for another 2 minutes, until the rice is coated in the oil and butter and just starting to smell nutty.

// Add the wine and stir until it has been fully absorbed. Mmmmmm. Fat little wine-and-butter-soaked rice. Now, one large ladle or so at a time, add the warm stock. It will sizzle and cover the rice and seem soupy. Stir pretty continuously until the stock has been absorbed, a couple of minutes. Then add another ladle and stir until absorbed. Repeat and repeat.

// **Reader, this will take somewhere around 20 to 30 minutes, but never fear because you are drinking a delicious glass of white wine and watching your show.** This might be the best portion of your day. Who murdered the eleven-year-old boy in the quiet British seaside town of Broadchurch? Will Detective Ellie Miller get to the bottom of it?? Well, you have at least 20 minutes to stand there and find out, and thank goodness for that wine, because the ending will lay you out flat.

// Your risotto is done when a cook's bite confirms the rice is still a little firm but not hard in the middle. You might use all the stock and you might not, because risotto does what it wants on any given day. (If you used it up and the rice still needs to cook a bit more, add hot water by the ladle until you get there.)

// Take the risotto off the heat and stir in the Parmesan, remaining 2 tablespoons butter, chives or parsley, and salt and pepper to taste. Here's where you add anything else you want to add (already cooked separately, if it needs to be cooked). This is the perfect food. Risotto is the coziest, creamiest, most comforting dish in the world, including Middle America.

Cacio e Pepe

This recipe is literally the reason I invented this chapter. It barely has any ingredients, you probably have them all, it takes 20 minutes from start to finish, and the magic element is water. I can't explain why this recipe works like a dream, but it does.

This is a classic Italian pasta dish, and *since you asked*, yes, I will tell you about the time I spent a week in Tuscany with my best friends and we bought basic bruschetta ingredients from the local market—vine-ripe tomatoes, homemade mozzarella, fresh basil, bakery bread, local olive oil and balsamic—and ate it for seven straight meals. Stop asking about my trip to Italy, you guys!

My point is this: food can be simple and still utterly divine. We have gotten real freaking precious about cooking, but our grandmas didn't *sous vide* their meat and *foam* their sauces. If this book was filled with a bunch of complicated recipes and mile-long ingredient lists, my grandma King would come back from the grave and haunt me in a clown costume. Everyone take it down a notch.

1 (16-ounce) box of sturdy pasta (I like spaghetti, but bucatini or linguine are also ZING)

2 to 3 tablespoons olive oil
—
6 tablespoons (¾ stick) butter

1 tablespoon (AT LEAST) freshly cracked black pepper

1 cup finely grated (good) Parmesan cheese (4 ounces)

1 cup finely grated (good) pecorino or Pecorino Romano cheese (4 ounces)

Chopped fresh parsley or basil, for serving (optional)

// I know what you're thinking. Why is this a recipe? It's basically butter + pepper + cheese pasta and now you know what *cacio e pepe* means. CHEESE AND PEPPER. And look, if cheese and pepper isn't good enough for you, I can no longer be of service here. These are two of my favorite food groups.

// Fill a big pot with water and bring it to a boil. Throw in two or three grabs of salt, and boil your pasta until it is about 3 minutes from done according to the package directions. (If you taste a strand, it should still have the barest *bite* in the middle.) This is the most important thing: scoop out 2 cups of that delicious salty starchy pasta water and set it aside before you drain the pasta. (If you don't do this, I will never speak to you again, because the recipe depends on that magic water.) Throw the pasta back in the pot, off the heat, and drizzle it with the olive oil.

// Meanwhile, in a large skillet, melt 4 tablespoons of the butter over medium heat and toss in the pepper. Yes, you need this much pepper. Look at the title of the recipe. If there are basically two important ingredients here, don't get suspicious about one of them. Toast that delicious pepper in that delicious butter for about 2 minutes (oh, do I ever love Kerrygold butter). (Because one time I was in Ireland with my best friends and we ate this brand . . . Stop asking me about my trip to Ireland, you guys!)

// Pour in 1 cup of that pasta water you saved and let it bubble up for a minute. Throw in the pasta and the rest of the butter and toss it all until the pasta is coated with the Pepper Butter™. Lower the heat and add the Parmesan and pecorino. Stir to coat. If this looks gummy, add more pasta water. (I always use the whole 2 cups.) The Magic Water™ brings the sauce together and makes it smooth and glossy.

// I like to toss fresh parsley or basil on top of this because it is so over-the-top rich and decadent, the fresh herbs pull you back from the brink of a heart attack. This needs to be served piping-hot and hopefully with a hunk of buttered French bread, a bright salad, and an additional crack of pepper. Your family will love this in a way that doesn't make sense for how simple and fast it is, but they don't need to know your tricks because they live in your house for free.

PAIRS PERFECTLY WITH a cold glass of Sancerre.

8

FOOD FOR WHEN YOU WANT TO SEEM FANCY

RECIPES THAT IMPRESS

Braised Short Ribs

3 tablespoons vegetable oil or grapeseed oil

5 pounds bone-in beef short ribs

Coarse salt and pepper

—

2 onions, chopped

4 medium carrots, chopped

4 celery stalks, chopped

—

3 tablespoons flour

1 tablespoon tomato paste

1 (750ml) bottle dry red wine (don't get weird with sweet wine, I'm serious)

—

½ cup fresh parsley

8 to 10 sprigs thyme

4 or 5 sprigs oregano

3 or 4 sprigs rosemary

2 or 3 bay leaves

1 whole head garlic, most of the oniony skin peeled off, halved crosswise

4 cups beef stock

GRAVY

2 tablespoons butter

3 tablespoons flour

½ to 1 cup heavy cream

TO GO WITH IT

White rice, cooked according to package directions

Or mashed potatoes

Or creamy grits

Or thickly sliced sourdough bread

Chopped fresh parsley

In *Anchorman 2*, Chani asks Brick, "What's your favorite food?" and his reply is: "Boiled."

Besides finding a way to work Kristen Wiig and Steve Carell into a cookbook, I also want to copy Brick's version of an answer, because my favorite food is "braised." Braised what? Yes.

Braising is a foolproof way to make inexpensive, tougher cuts of meat delectable, rich, ridiculous, pull-apart morsels of perfection. (I will use eight adjectives in a sentence *if I want to*, editors.) **This is the recipe to try if you feel a little dumb in the kitchen but want to be a star.** I am telling you that you cannot mess this up. You cannot. You could do half these steps out of order, leave stuff out, and get the measurements wrong, and it will still come out beautifully. Braising covers a multitude of sins.

SWAP

chuck roast for the short ribs (same weight).

// Preheat your oven to 350°F.

// Heat the oil in a large Dutch oven or heavy pot over medium-high heat. Season your short ribs pretty liberally on all sides with salt and pepper. In two batches, sear the short ribs on all four sides, around a minute per side. Yes, this step adds 10 minutes or so to your cooking time, but the sear does a special thing. I mean, I'm not a food chemist, but just *respect the process*. Transfer the seared short ribs to a plate and set aside.

// Now throw the onions, carrots, and celery into that delicious oil and fat and brown bits. Mmmmmm. Salt and pepper and stir a bit until the veggies start to get a little brown, 8 to 10 minutes. Add the flour and tomato paste and stir to coat. You want all that incorporated and cooked out a bit, around 3 minutes.

// Then add the whole bottle of wine. You read that right. Don't be precious about this. "But Jen, I don't want my kindergartner to get drunk off dinner." That's not how this works. If he wants to get sauced, he can dip into your bourbon after you go to bed like a normal kid; this wine will cook off its alcoholic tendencies and become a sauce fit for the gods. I would never lie to you. I care about your child's sobriety.

// Bring this to a boil, then lower the heat to a simmer. Let this mixture cook down and reduce for about 20 minutes.

RECIPE CONTINUES

// Add all the herbs, the garlic, and the stock and return the short ribs (and any meat juice on that plate!) to the pot. Bring back to a boil, cover, and put the whole thing in the oven for about 2½ hours. There really aren't enough superlatives for how this starts smelling. I like to braise when I'm cooking for guests, because the wow factor when they walk in the house distracts them from the pile of filthy teen shoes by the door. And I already told you it's foolproof, so all you can do with this recipe is win. You win like Beyoncé. You win like Oprah and Michelle Obama asked you to be their best friend.

// **Last step:** Remove the falling-apart short ribs to a plate and cover with foil. Set a strainer over a large bowl and carefully pour the sauce through the strainer, discarding the veggies and herb stalks. Let the strained sauce sit for a minute or two, then skim the fat off the top.

// **Now for the gravy:** In the same pot, melt the butter over medium heat, then whisk in the flour and cook, whisking, for about 2 minutes. Pour in the strained sauce and whisk until smooth. Cook for about 5 minutes, until the sauce thickens. Add the cream, whisk for 2 more minutes, then turn off the heat. Now you have a gravy that is too legit to quit.

// Put your "white carb" (mashies, rice, grits, thick bread) in a bowl, top with a couple of short ribs, then spoon the gravy aaaaaaaaall over the whole thing. If you want to be cute, sprinkle parsley on top. You'll write to me about this one.

> ### Note
>
> Pair with a hefty Cabernet. For a total bargain under $15, I love Dreaming Tree Wines.

PEPPERCORN-CRUSTED Beef Tenderloin WITH Horseradish Cream

This is not for just some random Wednesday night. This is for when you want to show off. Not a single thing we are about to undertake is remotely hard; it's one of the easiest recipes in the book, actually. But it FEELS SO FANCY. Think: New Year's Eve, Valentine's Day, perhaps Trisha and Garth are coming over for dinner. You cannot serve corn dogs to the king and queen of country music. They already have friends in low places. You will feed them a giant slab of expensive beef and quietly hum their songs, which will be super weird for everyone, but no one ever accused you of acting right.

Don't freak out when you see the price tag on a whole beef tenderloin (which I buy from a real old-timey butcher). You're basically buying uncut filets mignons for everyone, and frankly, Trisha and Garth deserve it. **Remember that you're showing off. This is not a humble meal.** You are trying to become their best friend. You are being impressive.

HORSERADISH CREAM SAUCE

1 cup sour cream

½ cup mayo

¼ cup prepared horseradish

1 tablespoon apple cider vinegar

3 tablespoons chopped fresh chives

Salt and pepper

---

1 (4-pound) whole beef tenderloin (take it out of the fridge an hour in advance)

2 tablespoons kosher salt

1 tablespoon sugar

½ cup whole black peppercorns, crushed with a rolling pin inside a plastic baggie

---

½ cup (1 stick) butter, melted

// Preheat your oven to 475°F. Get that oven hot.

// Meanwhile, whisk everything for the horseradish cream sauce together in a bowl. You can dial the bite up or down depending on the amount of horseradish you add. I love this ratio because it doesn't overpower the Fancy Meat, but you can adjust this however you prefer. Keep it in the fridge until you're ready to serve.

// Sprinkle the entire tenderloin with the salt and sugar. (I learned the sugar trick from Ree Drummond, who I forced to become my friend through the internet. It balances the extreme flavors of this rich meat and all that pepper.) Put the crushed peppercorns in a large dish or pan and press all sides of the seasoned tenderloin into them so the meat is coated. This will form a peppery, crunchy crust. Place the tenderloin on a rack, set it in a roasting pan, insert a meat thermometer, and put the whole thing in the oven. When the thermometer reads 120° to 125°F, you have a perfect rare/medium-rare tenderloin. This will take 20 to 25 minutes. (Little rare for you? Go another couple of minutes.)

RECIPE CONTINUES

// Take the tenderloin out and set it on a large platter. Pour the melted butter over the whole beautiful thing. Tent with foil and let it rest for at least 10 minutes before slicing.

// To serve, slice the tenderloin crosswise into 1-inch-thick slices and layer them around a big, lovely platter. In the middle of all that, set the bowl of horseradish cream sauce, which is so freaking perfect with this tenderloin—spicy, cold, and creamy against the rich beef—I honestly can't take it.

// I MEAN. If Trisha and Garth don't bust out their guitars and serenade you right at the dinner table, we'll switch back to corn dogs for the rest of our lives.

Note

LEFTOVERS

The WAY this hits the next morning, sliced razor-thin and piled next to your eggs. Or sliced razor-thin and layered over a crunchy Caesar salad. Or turned into a sandwich with sharp cheddar, sautéed onions, and Texadelphia Mustard Blend, I Guess (page 105).

1 whole chicken (These cost under $6. What is happening.)

Salt and pepper

1 lemon

1 whole head of garlic

1 package fresh thyme (around 8 to 10 sprigs)

5 tablespoons butter

2 onions, thickly sliced

———

3 tablespoons flour

1 cup half-and-half

FRIDAY NIGHT ROAST Chicken on THURSDAY

Ina Garten famously makes roast chicken on Fridays for Jeffrey. If my twenty-two references to her in this cookbook didn't make this clear, I am hopelessly devoted to Ina, but listen: she doesn't have kids, and thus her Friday nights look very, very, very different from mine. I am assuming her Friday nights are calm and simple as she and Jeffrey gently transition to their quiet weekend in the Hamptons. My Friday nights involve cranky, exhausted kids throwing themselves on the couch and saying "I don't even want a high school diploma!" and "My teacher MADE ME get a D!" and "Why don't we have any food in this house??" I have fourteen tasks unfinished from work, between four and seven random bonus kids drifting in the door, and we are D.O.N.E. and ordering numerous pizzas. I have no other Friday gear.

So this is your *Thursday* roast chicken recipe, which signals to your family "I still care about you today but the verdict will be out tomorrow night."

// That is literally it. Preheat your oven to 425°F.

// Rinse the inside and outside of your chick and pat it dry. Salt and pepper its insides a bunch, using about 1 tablespoon of each. I know this is weird. This is a good time to realize that we eat real animals, not just magical, boneless, precut breasts from some mythical creature who died of natural causes before its parts mysteriously dislodged, shrink-wrapped themselves, and landed in the meat department. I once thought watermelons grew underground, so I am not judging.

// Cut the lemon in half, cut crosswise through the head of garlic (don't worry about taking the skin off), grab however many sprigs of thyme you like, and shove all of that into the chicken's cavity. Melt 3 tablespoons of the butter, brush it all over the outside of the bird, then liberally salt and pepper. You can truss the chicken with twine if you'd like (google it), but I'm lazy. Put your buttered stuffed chicken in a roasting pan, breast-side up, scatter the onion all around it, and throw it in the oven. Roast, uncovered, for around 1 hour 15 minutes. There isn't the proper language to describe what this starts smelling like after around 30 minutes. Check it at 45 minutes or so and add a cup of water to the pan if your onions are starting to get too burny. (I realize that was a lot of words, but if you *edit the author's superfluous thoughts*, you'll see that your pre-roasting prep is like 6 minutes.)

// Anyhow, take the chicken out of the roasting pan when it's done, set it on a cutting board, and cover it with foil, and know that if you waste the pan drippings, I will never speak to you again. Set the pan on your stovetop over medium heat, throw in the remaining 2 tablespoons butter and the flour, and whisk it with all the pan drippings and onions for about 2 minutes. (Some people strain this, but that hurts my feelings.) Whisk in the half-and-half and cook for 2 to 3 more minutes, until the gravy has thickened up to your liking, then take it off the heat, and now you are a bona fide star.

// Serve your Thursday roast chicken and onion gravy with rice or mashed potatoes. Or with chips, because you've done enough here. Your kids are going to announce their impending school dropout plan tomorrow when they come home crabby and overstimulated, so don't waste too much time on them.

Notes

Goes great with a Sliced Wedge Salad (page 234).

Leftovers should absolutely become chicken salad (see page 112).

HONEY MUSTARD PECAN-CRUSTED
Salmon

I am *almost* embarrassed to include this recipe in this book. It doesn't even count as cooking, and the payoff is totally disproportionate. This is cheating. I have made this salmon for the last ten large dinner parties I've hosted because the prep is 5 minutes, the hardest step is melting butter, and everyone asks me for the recipe the next day and then the jig is up. If you're not eating salmon, it is time to get right with God. It is delicious. It is good for us. It saves us from taking fish oil. Here's your easiest, fastest, most delicious main dish this week.

HONEY MUSTARD

2 tablespoons Dijon mustard

2 tablespoons honey

2 tablespoons butter, melted

Pinch of salt

PECAN TOPPING

¼ cup bread crumbs or panko bread crumbs

¼ cup chopped fresh parsley

½ cup chopped pecans

1 plank skin-on fresh salmon from the seafood counter (around 2 pounds)

Salt and pepper

—

Fresh lemon juice

I LOVE THIS WITH

a bright, light Sauvignon Blanc. There's a Chilean Sauv Blanc called Matetic EQ Coastal that is divine with this.

// If you're like me, you have everything you need for this except the salmon and maybe some fresh parsley, so a 5-minute dash into the store has you in business. Get a whole plank of salmon from the fish guy in the seafood department. I have him cut it into six or seven portions because I am a lazy person and now my salmon is already portioned so I don't have to cut through the scaly skin on my kitchen counter. You can also not do this at all and just bake the whole plank. If our families cannot scoop their own portion of salmon onto their plates with a spatula, they need to enroll in life skills class.

ALSO, IF ONE WHOLE PLANK FEELS LIKE TOO MUCH:

1. You'll want to cook twice as much as you need so you can have some tomorrow when it is still just as tasty over your salad or tucked into tortillas or just eaten out of the Tupperware container.

2. I have no idea how to not cook an absurd amount of food. I have five kids and always have extra kids and also want leftovers and just make your peace with it.

// Preheat your oven to 400°F and line a baking sheet with parchment paper or foil.

// In a small bowl, mix the honey mustard ingredients until smooth. Stick this in the fridge for 10 minutes or so to slightly firm up. In another bowl, mix together the pecan topping ingredients.

// Rinse and pat the salmon dry, then salt and pepper the flesh side. Brush on the honey mustard pretty thick. Coat with the pecan mixture and pat that down. Set the salmon on your prepared baking sheet and bake for around 20 minutes (you could also grill this!), until flaky and opaque in the thickest part.

// When you take the salmon out of the oven, squeeze a bit of lemon over the top if you have it.

// Your children might look at this and ask if they can take "all that weird stuff off." Then you'll make them eat it as is because you are not raising dum-dums that won't try good food, and then they'll love it and get seconds and eat it until it is gone and you won't even manage to take a pic for Instagram. The tangy mustard, sweet honey, crunchy pecan mix, and toasted bread crumbs are just magic.

// We almost exclusively eat this with Sydney's Favorite Salad (page 228), and if you make this for guests, they will be embarrassingly impressed unless they hate seafood in which case you need to reevaluate that friendship anyway. What on earth. You are telling me you hate fried shrimp? You hate sushi?? Good day to you, sir. I SAID GOOD DAY.

CRAB Cakes

WITH Lemon Caper Butter Sauce

½ cup mayo

1 large egg, beaten

1 tablespoon Dijon mustard

1 tablespoon Worcestershire

1 teaspoon hot sauce

20 saltine crackers, crushed into fine crumbs

1 pound jumbo lump crabmeat (the best version is refrigerated by the seafood counter), picked over for any teeth-breaking shells

LEMON CAPER BUTTER SAUCE

3 tablespoons butter, plus 2 tablespoons cold butter

3 tablespoons capers

Juice of ½ lemon

Salt and pepper

3 tablespoons heavy cream

½ cup chopped fresh parsley

—

¼ cup canola oil

Salt

I have two well-known weaknesses: egg salad and crab cakes. Like, I'm not kidding you. If either of these things are ever on a menu, there is a 100% chance I'm ordering them. I just really like food bound in mayonnaise (Exhibit A: "Mayo-Based-'Salad' Sandwiches" are an entire entry starting on page 110).

We need to have a quick talk about mayo. **If you ever use Miracle Whip in these recipes, I am going to sue you for libel.** Don't get me started on low-fat mayo or tofu mayo or some other weird thing. Give me Duke's mayo or give me death. I realize Mayo Brand Loyalty™ is regional, but here in the South, I don't even know why they stock any other brands. They just sit there dusty while Duke's flies off the shelves faster than deviled eggs at a church potluck (made with Duke's, of course). These are my mayonnaise values, and I don't want to say anyone else is wrong, but they are.

Moving on.

I am so excited for you to make this recipe. I feel like eight out of ten of you have never made crab cakes, and once you see how easy these are, and how fancy you feel, and how DELISH they are made right in your little kitchen, you're going to be so tickled with yourself. Some crab cake recipes are full of mess. Extra this and that, modern additions, flavor twists: "Enjoy our award-winning crab cakes made with almond paste and crushed Cheerios!" But I like pure crab cakes without weird fillers, crab cakes that I would be proud to serve to the grandmother of the governor of Maryland, and this is it. This dish cannot be improved upon.

SERVE WITH
rémoulade (see page 127).

// In a medium bowl, whisk together the mayo, egg, Dijon, Worcestershire, and hot sauce until smooth. Put the crackers in a large plastic baggie and crush them with your rolling pin until the crumbs are really fine. This is satisfying. Enjoy yourself. Gently add the crackers and crab to the mayo mix. You don't want to break the crab up into little pieces, so be very precious with this. Fold it all together until it is totally mixed. Cover and put in your fridge for at least an hour.

// For the sauce, melt the 3 tablespoons butter over medium heat until it foams. Add the capers and sauté in the butter for 30 seconds. Add the lemon juice and salt and pepper and stir until the sauce is reduced by a third, around 2 minutes. Remove from the heat, add the 2 tablespoons cold butter and the cream, and stir continuously until the butter has melted and the sauce is shiny and thickened. Stir in the parsley. (This will become a go-to sauce for you because lemon and butter are soul mates.)

// In a heavy skillet or cast-iron pan, heat the oil over medium heat until shimmering. Scoop ⅓ cup of the crab mix into your hand and gently shape it into a patty, lightly packed and about 1½ inches thick. Set aside on a plate and repeat with the rest of the crab mix (this will make 8 to 10 cakes). Fry the crab cakes on one side until deeply golden, 4 to 5 minutes, then flip and fry the other side. Transfer to a platter, sprinkle with salt, drizzle with the lemon caper butter sauce, and serve immediately.

// WHY IS THIS SO GOOD. I can feel the warm glow of approval from the governor's grandmother as we speak. Put this stuff on your grocery list and make crab cakes this very week.

JEFF'S MOM'S Oil-Poached Fish WITH Soy, Ginger, and Scallions

4 large cod fillets (you could use snapper or halibut, or any good white fish), about 5 ounces each

Salt and pepper

¼ cup extra-virgin olive oil

½ cup sliced scallions

2 tablespoons chopped fresh garlic

2 tablespoons chopped fresh ginger

—

¼ cup soy sauce

One of my best people in the whole earth is Jeff Chu, a Chinese American theologian obsessed with farming. If you can find an Ordained Gaysian (his term) who loves you, I highly recommend it.

When Jeff and his husband, Tristan, spent several weeks in Austin last year, I lured him into my kitchen. What this meant pragmatically is that Jeff bought and brought all the ingredients to make a Chinese feast, and I simply provided the burners, pots, and wine.

Me: "JEFF. This is a lot of groceries. What are you making??"

Jeff: "My mom says you make one less dish than the number of people."

Me: "There are eight of us, Jeff."

Jeff: "We are having eleven dishes. It's a flexible rule."

Reader, WE DID. We had eleven whole dishes, and this is no hint of a lie. I did some sous cheffing while Tristan drank wine at the kitchen bar, as that is his personal spiritual gift. My mom and I are *still* talking about this dreamy culinary experience, but Jeff's mom's oil-poached fish almost made me faint. I need you to confirm right now that you will believe me and make this.

I asked Jeff for this recipe and he sent me a hot mess of zero quantities and vague instructions. I had to go back and look at the pictures I took that night. (*Was it two scallions? Twelve??*) Thus, I was *forced* to put this into test-kitchen mode and make it ten times more than necessary, because this is so good, you will die.

// Look at how easy this is going to be! This is the shortest ingredient list in this book, with the absolute highest impact.

// Preheat your oven to 400°F.

// Rinse the cod, pat it dry, season both sides with salt and pepper, and set it aside.

// In a skillet, combine the oil, scallions, garlic, and ginger and cook over medium heat until fragrant and softened, around 5 minutes. Remove from the heat.

// Jeff cooked his fish in a foil packet, so that is what the rest of us will do: Place the cod in the middle of a large piece of foil on a baking sheet. Fold the sides of the foil up enough to keep it all in, pour the hot, flavored oil evenly over the fish, then bring the edges of the foil together and crimp to seal them. (Not only is this divine, there is no cleanup.)

// Pop it into the oven for 10 to 12 minutes (15 for super thick pieces of fish). Carefully transfer the fish to a lovely serving dish. Drizzle evenly with the soy sauce, then pour EVERY OUNCE of the scallion-garlic-ginger oil left in the foil packet over it. If you spill one drop, so help me. The cooking method here ensures the fish is utterly tender and deeply flavored.

// I don't know what to say. I wish Jeff was your friend too, but you got the second best thing with this recipe. **Food made with love by beloved friends is the best food.** We infuse our dishes with affection for the people we make them for. I'm convinced love makes food taste better.

Notes

Pairs well with good company. Obey accordingly.

Goes great with delicious Glazed Garlic Green Beans. No, that recipe isn't in this cookbook. Use your google.

GRILLED SHRIMP
WITH
Hot Honey AND Coconut Rice

Pairs Well With a tart margarita on the rocks rimmed with salt.

It is probably apparent at this point that my favorite flavor is Hot™. I've never met a spice I didn't like, and my tip-top way to eat hot food is paired with sweet. Sweet-and-savory and sweet-and-spicy is my flavor profile, and I cannot be reformed. I was literally meant to be Southeast Asian but I was accidentally born in Kansas.

My girlfriends and I recently had lunch on the river at Neighbor's Kitchen & Yard in Bastrop, and naturally, I ordered a pizza called "hot l'il honey" because it met my requirements: spicy salami, sweet cherry peppers, and—here is the kicker—a hot habanero honey drizzle. I had no idea what that was, but I was damn sure about to find out. I freaked out so disproportionately that I was forced to share my hot l'il honey because the girls got swept up in my enthusiasm, so the moral of that story is, don't tell your friends when your food is good.

So enthused were we about the hot honey, we cornered not one, not two, but three Neighbor's employees, including the owner, to secure the details. We were delightfully told three different versions, so the six of us went home and put all three into the test kitchen because we were unable to live without the hot honey in our daily lives. I give you the winner. You will never be the same. You will only use 3 tablespoons of this honey for the recipe, so PLEASE ENJOY the remainder of your jar paired with anything I've suggested on page 222. Please drizzle it over pizza. Please.

HOT HONEY

1 (12-ounce) jar good local honey

1 tablespoon water

1 habanero chile, stemmed and cut in half

COCONUT RICE

1 (13.5-ounce) can coconut milk (fuuuuuuuull-fat)

1½ cups coconut water

2 teaspoons salt, plus more if needed

2 cups uncooked jasmine rice

—

1 cup diced fresh mango

1 cup chopped fresh cilantro

GLAZE

3 tablespoons soy sauce

2 tablespoons fresh lime juice

Pinch of salt

—

1 pound deveined large shrimp, peeled but tails left on

Grapeseed or other neutral oil, for the grill

Chopped fresh cilantro, for garnish

1 cup chopped roasted peanuts, for garnish

// Let's get that hot honey going. This took me soooooooo many times to get right, but this exact version is IT. Sorry to be weirdly specific, but in this case, I must because eight of my test versions were so hot, they actually would have killed your family. (In my first attempt, I used five habaneros like a sociopath.) Speaking of murder, be sure to wear kitchen gloves when you handle these no-joke peppers, or you'll touch your eyes later and wish you were dead.

RECIPE CONTINUES

// In a small saucepan, combine the honey, halved habanero, and water. Turn the heat to high and just stand there looking at it like a stalker. Right when it comes to a full bubbly boil, set a timer for 1 minute. At the buzzer, take it off the heat and immediately strain it through a fine-mesh sieve into a mason jar, discarding the habanero and any seeds. Let the honey cool and then get ready to party, because this hot honey is lit.

// Bring the coconut milk, coconut water, and salt to a boil in a saucepan, then stir in the rice. Turn the heat down to low, cover, and cook for about 20 minutes. (Or throw all this into the rice cooker someone gave you for your wedding, which sat in an unopened box for fifteen years until you dragged it out some random day and now use it twice a week. The marriage didn't make it but the rice cooker did. Bloop.) Remove from the heat and let the rice sit, covered, for 5 minutes, then stir in the mango and cilantro. Grab a quick taste and add more salt if needed.

// Fire up your grill to medium. While you're waiting for things to heat up, make your glaze: In a small bowl, whisk together 3 tablespoons of the hot honey, the soy sauce, lime juice, and salt until combined. (You can dial any of these flavors up or down. Taste and see what you like.)

// Slide your shrimp onto skewers. Lightly oil the grates, then place the skewers on the grill and brush them liberally with the hot honey glaze. Cook for 2 minutes, then flip and brush the glaze on the other side. Grill for another 2 minutes, or until the shrimp are no longer translucent.

// Build your gorgeous bowl: coconut rice with that delicious mango, glazed grilled shrimp, and, because you love yourself and deserve good things, another little drizzle of hot honey. Sprinkle with more cilantro and the peanuts. This dish is the reason God invented summer dinner parties.

What else can you drizzle with your hot honey?

+ **Homemade biscuits or cornbread**
+ **Grilled peaches or pineapple**
+ **Ice cream**
+ **Wings**
+ **Fried chicken and waffles**
+ **Pizza**
+ **Glazed ham**
+ **Roasted Brussels sprouts or green beans**
+ **Grilled salmon or ribs**
+ **Inside a grilled cheese**
+ **On buttered toast with a fried egg on top**
+ **In a million cocktails**

Pork Tenderloin

with Orange-Chipotle Honey Glaze

Fine. I have a real problem with pork chops. I find them in general flavorless, dry, and usually overcooked. They are so very uninteresting. The only ones I ever fully loved were deep-fried and covered in gravy, but what wouldn't be good like that? That doesn't even count as real food; that's just breading and sauce. The Other White Meat is boring and I don't love it.

Except I totally love pork tenderloin. I CONTAIN MULTITUDES.

What pork chops sacrifice in flavor, tenderloin makes up for in, well, tenderness, which I assume is why God named it "tenderloin." **This dish is the answer to the age-old question: How can I have an elegant dinner party without working hard?** It's not that we're fancy. It's that we want to *seem* fancy, just like we teach our children. Integrity doesn't matter, kids; it's what's on the outside that counts.

I give you herb-crusted pork tenderloin with orange-chipotle honey glaze. This is an absolute crowd-pleaser and gorgeous to look at. Almost every ingredient is listed in the title so why do we even need a recipe? See also: why do I put the entire ingredient list in the title?

1 pound pork tenderloin

Salt and pepper

2 tablespoons Dijon mustard

3 tablespoons olive oil

1 tablespoon soy sauce

—

3 tablespoons chopped fresh thyme

3 tablespoons chopped fresh rosemary, plus extra sprigs for serving, if you want

1 bunch parsley, chopped

ORANGE-CHIPOTLE HONEY GLAZE

1 canned chipotle pepper in adobo sauce, diced (no one will be mad if you add a spoonful of that sauce, too)

3 tablespoons honey

⅓ cup fresh orange juice

1 tablespoon Dijon mustard

Pinch of salt

// Preheat your oven to 400°F.

// Trim any tendrils of fat or leftover membrane off the tenderloin. You want it looking like a naked baby. Give the baby a quick sprinkle of salt and pepper. In a small bowl, whisk up the Dijon, 1 tablespoon of the olive oil, and the soy sauce and then brush this mix liberally all over the tenderloin.

// Throw all your fresh herbs into the food processor and whiz away. You want this herb mix pretty finely processed because it'll stick better that way and you won't end up eating big chunks of rosemary or whatever. No food processor? Just finely chop it all up with a knife.

// Right on your cutting board, spread the herbs out and roll the marinated tenderloin in them like a naked baby in a bathtub. Coat all sides with that yumminess.

RECIPE CONTINUES

// In a skillet, heat the remaining 2 tablespoons olive oil over medium-high heat, then sear the tenderloin for about 2 minutes per side. You aren't cooking this through, just searing that herb crust and locking in the moisture. Put the tenderloin on a baking sheet, slide it into the oven, and bake for 15 to 25 minutes. Cooking time will vary from kitchen to cut of meat to oven, so use a meat thermometer so you don't give your guests salmonella as a party favor. When the internal temp reads 145°F, you're there. Take the pork out of the oven and let it rest for 10 minutes.

// Which is the perfect time to whip up your glazy, sticky sauce. Combine all the glaze ingredients in a small saucepan and bring to a boil over medium heat. Lower the heat and cook, stirring, for another 2 minutes or so, until the glaze thickens up, then take it off the heat.

// The most gorgeous way to plate this is family-style on a big platter. Cut the tenderloin into 1-inch-thick slices and layer them like toppled dominoes. Get real freaking generous spooning the orange-chipotle honey glaze all over the slices. That sauce is boss, man. Tuck a few whole sprigs of rosemary around the edges of the platter, because you are being fancy. Pork chops can't compete with this, folks.

Note

Chop any leftovers into a frittata tomorrow morning with onions, bell peppers, and Monterey Jack cheese.

9

FOOD THAT GOES NEXT TO YOUR FOOD

SIDES & SALADS

Sydney's Favorite Salad

In general, I'm not a huge fan of cold food. I like eating things that feel cooked. I want warm food that could burn me. I like melty, toasty, oozy, saucy. Here are my weird exceptions:

1. I absolutely love cold spaghetti the next day. I eat it straight out of the Tupperware like a caveman. I like it cold almost better than hot.

2. I love cold pizza. Because I'm a normal person.

3. I love coleslaw, but it needs to be paired with hot food. By itself, it is a bit of a sad panda.

4. I love cold dips, but I don't know if that counts as food.

So it was no joy to me that the salad lobby really sunk its claws in. Our moms never ate salads. They certainly weren't going to order one at a restaurant when they could choose meatloaf instead. Salads are so medium. I mean, they're fine. But they aren't quesadillas.

But for some reason, I heart-emoji-love this one. This is a copycat salad from one of our favorite restaurants in Austin: Satellite. We went there after church for a decade, and my daughter Sydney and I ordered this salad (add grilled salmon) virtually every time. I ordered a salad! On purpose! And paid for it with money I earned! We workshopped the champagne vinaigrette until we got it exactly right, and this salad will make me think of Sydney for the rest of my life.

1 cup red wine vinegar

1 tablespoon sugar

1 tablespoon salt

½ red onion, thinly sliced

CHAMPAGNE VINAIGRETTE

1 garlic clove, minced

2 tablespoons Dijon mustard

2 tablespoons honey

¼ cup champagne vinegar

¼ cup extra-virgin olive oil

Juice of ½ lemon

Salt and pepper

1 head butter lettuce (Is it little? Use 2 heads.), rustically torn into large pieces

1 avocado, sliced into beautiful avocado fans

1 (8-ounce) container ripe cherry tomatoes, halved

1 cucumber, peeled and chopped

4 ounces crumbled Gorgonzola cheese

4 ounces honey-roasted pecans, coarsely chopped

Kosher salt and cracked pepper

// In a container with a lid, whisk together the red wine vinegar, sugar, and salt until the sugar and salt have dissolved. Add the onion, cover, and put this in the fridge for at least an hour to quick pickle. You could do this the day before, too.

// Put all the champagne vinaigrette ingredients into a jar with a lid and shake until totally mixed. Give it a taste. You might want this adjusted. I like my dressing vinegar-forward, but a little more olive oil or honey would mellow it out. You could make this when you pickle the onions, and stick it in the fridge to really come together.

// I build this salad in a wide, shallow salad platter. (Who am I kidding? I build all salads in that platter because I don't like how the fancy ingredients fall to the bottom in a big bowl so only the last person served gets the good stuff while I only get the lettuce on top since I got in line first because I was hungry.)

// I like to dress all the lettuce right before serving, which is a hot take in my family since we usually like different dressings. Don't make four times as much as you plan to eat, because dressed salad has a shelf life, and that shelf is through the end of dinner. So toss only the lettuce in the dressing until evenly coated (you probably won't use the whole amount; you can always add more dressing but you can't fix an overdressed salad).

// Now your lettuce is perfectly flavored. Butter lettuce is such a dreamy lettuce. It is so soft and pleasing and pretty to look at. And when you buy it whole, it comes still attached to the root. We are like farmers! Over the lettuce, evenly scatter the fanned avocado (fancy!), cherry tomatoes, cucumber, Gorgonzola, pickled red onion, and honey-roasted pecans. Drizzle the toppings with a bit more dressing. Sprinkle with crunchy salt and cracked pepper. Set the extra dressing on the side for your people who prefer salad soup.

// **This is a perfect partner for literally any recipe in the Fancy section, but Sydney and I recommend the salmon on page 213.** Cold salad! It's what's for dinner! On purpose!

Winter Panzanella

The first time I understood that bread could be the main ingredient in a salad, I decided to become a vegetarian for two whole hours. It didn't last because I love cheeseburgers and fried chicken and bacon and pulled pork and hot dogs, which [[checks notes]] are "problematic" for vegetarians, but if I could eat bread salad every day, I might still consider it, if I could eat meat on the side.

Related: my daughter Sydney became a vegetarian when she was twelve, which I thought was a phase since she is the granddaughter of a cattle rancher and our shared family value is Things Made with Meat, but it stuck. She is a grown-ass adult and hasn't had a bite of beef in ten years. HOWEVER, she called me her freshman year in college and said:

"Mom, I've done something, and I don't know how you're going to take it."

Reader, there are several ways you don't want your spawn to begin a conversation, and this is one of them. While my mind Rolodexed through the possibilities—she dropped out of school, she wrecked her car, she got a thigh tattoo, she voted Libertarian—Sydney cleared her throat and whispered:

"I ate Chick-fil-A yesterday, and it was as delicious as I remembered."

So now she's what we call a "Chick-fil-A Vegetarian" who eats her nuggs on the regular, and this is very on brand for our family because we struggle to follow rules. Let us live, America.

Back to this recipe. Panzanella is basically crouton salad. Its most popular iteration is made in the summer with juicy tomatoes, crunchy cukes, briny olives, and all the fresh tastes of July. It has a winter cousin that I love just as much but that doesn't get the attention, so I'm pulling her into rotation as a contender. I've done this a dozen different ways, and they're all perfect—because a salad with bread as its main ingredient cannot *not* be perfect—but here is my fave.

DRESSING

¼ cup apple cider vinegar or red wine vinegar

½ cup olive oil

1 tablespoon Dijon mustard

1 tablespoon fresh lemon juice

Pinch of salt

Pinch of pepper

CROUTONS

5 to 6 cups cubed two-day-old bread (cut the crust off before cubing it into bite-size pieces)

4 tablespoons (½ stick) butter, melted

¼ cup olive oil

¼ cup grated Parmesan cheese

2 tablespoons chopped fresh thyme

2 tablespoons chopped garlic

Salt and pepper

—

1 small red onion, thinly sliced

4 cups cubed peeled butternut squash (small bite-size cubes)

4 leeks, white and light green parts only, thinly sliced into rounds and rinsed well to remove grit

¼ cup olive oil

Salt and pepper

—

2 tablespoons chopped fresh sage

1 cup chopped fresh parsley

¼ cup dried cranberries

½ cup crumbled fresh goat cheese (or feta or blue cheese)

RECIPE CONTINUES

// I am so happy just looking at this list. I love everything on it. My sister Lindsay asked me one time what my favorite herb was, and I said thyme, and she said thyme isn't really anyone's *favorite* herb but since I just said it was mine, there went her "no one" theory.

// Get those dressing ingredients into a mason jar, shake it real good, and stick it in the fridge. It gets better as it sits, so give it a minute to get its life right.

// **Now for the croutons:** Preheat your oven to 350°F.

// On a large baking sheet, toss your bread cubes evenly with the rest of the crouton ingredients ("melted butter through salt and pepper"). Make sure they're in a single layer, then toast them in the oven for 15 to 20 minutes, until they're browning and crunchy and smell super delicious. Take them out and let them cool in your salad bowl.

// Turn your oven up to 400°F and, on the same baking sheet, toss your onion, butternut squash, and leeks with the olive oil and salt and pepper to taste. (Quick leek thing: These are serious root veggies, and dirt just loves to live inside their layers. After you slice your leeks, rinse them in a colander so you don't accidentally make Dirt Salad.) Roast these delectable winter vegetables for 30 to 40 minutes, until the squash is fork-tender. Give the whole pan a shake and toss halfway through. Take it out and let it cool slightly.

// I love a shallow, wide serving bowl for this so the croutons don't get buried and soggy. Plus, it is SO GORGEOUS to look at, I want the largest possible surface area so I can Salad Brag. Gently toss the roasted veggies, croutons, sage, and parsley with the dressing (as much or as little as you want), then scatter the cranberries and goat cheese over the top. Crack some delicious pepper over the whole thing.

// Excuse me, but this is dinner. This is my entire meal. You can bulk it up with shredded roast chicken or grilled shrimp, or you can just grab a fork and get down to business. Ugh, this is so good. I am furious I don't have panzanella made right this second.

Note

Cube stale bread and freeze it so you'll have almost-ready-made croutons at all times.

Sliced Wedge Salad

Wedge salads are my worldview. I pledge allegiance to their flag, one nation under blue cheese crumbles. I am their patriot and partisan pundit. They have but one flaw: in their traditional form, I can never get the dressing and crumbles and bacon and goop into the innards enough. The outside of the wedge? I am a straight-ticket voter. The inside of the iceberg wedge? FILIBUSTER.

This is a solution created by the simpleton writing this cookbook, meaning my primary legislative agenda was "how can I get more goop and less lettuce?" because health is important to me. These look just as beautiful and won't leave you with a mouthful of plain iceberg, which is as depressing as the Electoral College.

Creamy Blue Cheese dressing (page 98) OR Spicy Ranch dressing (page 98)

1 head iceberg lettuce

4 ounces blue cheese crumbles (or Gorgonzola or feta)

12 ounces bacon, chopped, cooked until crunchy, and drained

1 (12-ounce) container cherry tomatoes (1½ cups), halved or quartered

1 cup thinly sliced scallions

Sea salt and pepper

// Why is this so delicious? Look at the list; it is so whatever. But for some reason, wedge salads taste damn good, and they have a restaurant quality that feels fancy.

// Get that dressing made first and stick it in your fridge to get awesome.

// You want that lettuce crispy cold, so don't arrange this until right before serving. Rather than quarter your iceberg for a traditional wedge, cut it in half through the root and triangle out the core from each half with your knife. Then, working with one half at a time, hold the iceberg upright like the letter *D* and cut it into 1-inch-thick slices, keeping the layers intact.

// I'm a huge fan of plating this in advance for your eaters. Part of its charm is how pretty it looks, and you don't want those fools leaving off the tomatoes or blue cheese. Use a shallow, wide serving platter and lay the lettuce slices side by side. Then scatter them with the blue cheese crumbles, bacon, cherry tomatoes, and scallions. And yes, drizzle them all with the homemade blue cheese dressing, because if people don't like blue cheese, they need to get some counseling. (If you're trying to be ACCOMMODATING, you can have spicy ranch as an option too.) Sprinkle the whole platter with sea salt and tons of fresh black pepper, and put this gorgeous dish on your table.

// There is not a single recipe in the "Food for When You Want to Seem Fancy" chapter that wouldn't love this salad as its side piece.

Perfect Onion Rings

A pretty decent way to be a hero tonight is to make homemade onion rings. I am 93% sure you have everything you need. And by the way, your kids don't have to like onions to like onion rings. If they like "fried" as a food group, they will love these. Fried food is one of my core values, and this is how you know you can trust my leadership.

High-temp oil, for frying

—

4 cups milk

3 tablespoons white vinegar

3 cups flour

¼ cup seasoning blend (whatever you like!)

—

3 large onions

// Put 3 inches of oil into a big, heavy pot and heat it to 375°F. This is no lie: I was cleaning out the bottom of some assorted bottles to make this once, and I used a combination of avocado oil, canola oil, and coconut oil. The moral of this story is, who cares? But do not fry these in olive oil because that is a low-temperature oil and honestly? It is really best uncooked or used as a finishing oil, but I'm not in the mood for a brawl, so let's leave that for another day. DON'T @ ME, RACHAEL RAY.

// Pour your milk and vinegar into a bowl. (This is what to do when you don't have buttermilk, because you are smart.) Dump your flour into a shallow dish. (Like a bit more texture? Add some cornmeal to your flour.) I add 2 tablespoons of the seasoning blend to the buttermilk and another 2 tablespoons to the flour. And those seasonings are whatever I grab. I like salt and pepper plus Cajun seasoning, but if you are precious about spice, use steak seasoning or Lawry's or Uncle Chris' or just whatever you want. Fried onions are a very accommodating home for flavor.

// Preheat your oven to 250°F and set a wire rack over a rimmed baking sheet. Slice your onions crosswise into rings. If your family is weird about onions, slice them thin. Dunk them in the buttermilk, tong them into the seasoned flour, then slide them into the hot oil. Work in batches—don't crowd these too much. Fry them until they are GORGEOUS BROWN, 4 to 5 minutes per batch (no need to flip), then remove them with tongs or a large slotted spoon, put them on that rack, salt them like you have a sodium deficiency, and keep them warm in the oven until you've gotten through all the batches.

// If this is all you serve for dinner, only God can judge you. I sure wouldn't. Onion Ring Dinner sounds like #goals. Especially with a mountain of ketchup. (I eat ketchup in kindergartener quantities.) But obviously these love Diner Cheeseburger Sliders (page 155). Or Homemade Corn Dogs (page 138). Maybe Peppercorn-Crusted Beef Tenderloin (page 207) if you're in a real fancy steak house mood. Make these tonight, then update your Instagram bio to "Queen."

HACKED Uchi Brussels Sprouts

In Austin, we got real damn lucky that chef Tyson Cole opened Uchi on South Lamar. (One mile from my church. Uchi and Austin New Church have such a shared connection to God, I don't know how else to convince you that Jesus is real. Maybe these Brussels will do the trick.) You can never get in, you need rezzies a hundred years in advance, and you will mortgage your house to pay the bill. AND YET WE ALL DO IT. Happily. Take my money, Tyson. Take my car payment, Uchi.

Inarguably, one of its most celebrated menu items is the Brussels sprouts. Guys, I will tell you straight up: the juice is worth the squeeze here. I will also tell you this: when my friends and I set out to copycat this recipe ten years ago, we discovered an alarming fact. Do you know what Uchi calls the famous glaze that makes these undefeatable? "Fish caramel." This is so upsetting. Where is your publicist. We can never call something fish caramel and expect its appeal to be evident. No to the fish caramel. I mean, yes to it, obviously, because it is the most delicious glaze in the known universe, but no to its branding. I'm here to rescue it from a PR nightmare.

These are the living best.

Note
NO DAMNS ALTERNATIVE

Mix ½ cup sweet chili sauce with 2 tablespoons soy sauce for a quicker glaze!

---

1 pound Brussels sprouts

3 tablespoons high-temp oil (grapeseed is my go-to)

Salt and pepper

GLAZE

3 garlic cloves, chopped

1 tablespoon chopped fresh ginger

3 tablespoons soy sauce

2 tablespoons maple syrup

Juice of ½ lemon

1 tablespoon fish sauce

1 tablespoon sriracha

Salt and pepper

// Crank your oven to 425°F.

// Trim your Brussels by cutting off the bottoms, then cutting them into halves or quarters depending on how large they are. Look at it this way: the more surface area there is, the more crispy they get, and the more glaze they soak up. So chop chop, home chef. Toss the Brussels with the oil and salt and pepper to taste on a baking sheet, then roast for 30 to 40 minutes or so, tossing them halfway through. You want these brown and crispy. Otherwise? Might as well serve the boiled Brussels tragedy our moms fed us in the '80s. What a freaking nightmare. What culinary abuse. Worse than calling something "fish caramel."

// While the Brussels are roasting, let's reduce that glaze. From the ingredient list, throw "garlic through salt and pepper" into a saucepan and cook over medium heat, stirring, until reduced and thickened, around 10 minutes. Take it off the heat and let it thicken up even a bit more.

// When the Brussels are beautiful browned things, take them out of the oven, drizzle liberally with the glaze (I am rebranding the fish caramel), and put them back in the oven for another 5 minutes. Take them out, toss to coat, and serve immediately in a wide, shallow bowl. If you have any sauce left, serve it on the side for additional drizzling.

// This is the perfect side food. Tyson is right to charge $10 for a tiny dish of them. I would pay $20 for four bites without batting an eye, but now you can make an entire pan at home for around $5. I would serve these with any recipe in this book. I'd serve them next to the Blueberry Almond French Toast Bake (page 45), I swear to Abraham.

GRANDMA KING'S
CARROTS

When I told my family I was writing a cookbook, they said two things:

1. "Wow. The cookbook industry has no standards."

2. "You have to include Grandma's carrots."

And I am, and I don't care that this is a trash recipe. This was on every, and I mean *every*, holiday table throughout my entire childhood. As the four of us grew up and flew the coop, we all called home for this recipe to serve to our new mothers-in-law or boyfriends or roommates. Wait. Not true. The baby never called home for Grandma's carrots because he is spoiled and someone always makes these for him. When you are the youngest boy with three older sisters, you merely have to *think* of something you want and one of us will procure it. (Once, before we all moved to Austin, one sister called me to talk shit about the other sister after Thanksgiving: "I hate when we are all together. Cortney just HOGS Drew the entire time!" LOL. We need counseling.)

Get ready, everyone.

1 (32-ounce) bag carrots

—

1 (16-ounce) brick Velveeta

1 cup half-and-half

6 tablespoons (¾ stick) butter, plus 4 tablespoons (½ stick) butter, melted

1 tablespoon salt

1 teaspoon black pepper

1 teaspoon cayenne pepper (or more if you like)

2 cups Pepperidge Farm herb-seasoned stuffing

Note You can 100% dress this up with fresh herbs or onions or toasted nuts, of course.

// I laughed the entire time I typed this list. Wtf.

// Let's talk about the carrots first. I love my grandma King. I do. God rest her blessed memory. God love her costume jewelry, her acrylic nails, her floor-length mink, and her basement full of Chico's tunics. But Grandma used canned carrots in her recipe, and it was a bridge too far when we re-created this as adults. Vegetables I will allow out of a can: Le Sueur peas, pickled asparagus, corn. That's it. That's the list. This feels generous, because we grew up with Veg-All, may God have mercy on our souls.

// Preheat your oven to 350°F and butter a 9 x 13-inch casserole dish.

// Bring a pot of salted water to a boil. Peel and slice your carrots on an angle, not too thick. **Oh! You are forbidden to use baby carrots. Those are an affront to nature.** What even the heck with fake baby carrots. Drop your sliced Carrots From The Earth™ into that boiling water and cook until firmish-tender, 12 to 15 minutes, then drain.

// Meanwhile, put the Velveeta, half-and-half, and the 6 tablespoons butter into a microwave-safe bowl and zap it for a minute at a time, stirring after each zap, until you have a creamy, smooth cheese concoction, 3 to 4 minutes total. We tried to get fancy with this one year and used real cheese, and it was an abomination. You will use the Velveeta and you will like it.

// In your buttered casserole dish, spread a layer of carrots, then follow with a sprinkling of salt and black pepper and cayenne, a layer of the stuffing (use 1 cup here), a layer of the cheese sauce, the rest of the carrots plus S&P and cayenne, then pour the rest of the cheese mix all over the whole thing. Bake, uncovered, for 25 minutes. Take it out and switch the oven to broil. Top the casserole with the remaining 1 cup stuffing mix, drizzle with the 4 tablespoons melted butter, and put it under the broiler on the middle rack for 3 to 5 minutes, until the stuffing is browned and crunchy.

// Whatever, haters! Don't you dare knock Grandma King's cheese carrots until you've tried them. Sure, I considered elevating this recipe with garlic or fresh herbs or some sophisticated substitution, but guess what? I prefer the 1980s green bean casserole with cream of mushroom soup and canned fried onions over the food blogger versions, too. Get out of here with "pickled shallots" on top. I can't wait for y'all to make these and love them. I cannot quit laughing. I'll make these until I die.

Grilled Avocado
BALSAMIC Bruschetta

Maybe ten years ago, I went to a gorgeous outdoor wedding in the Hill Country where Melissa the Bride wore cowboy boots with her designer gown. It was super fancy but also there were horses. This is all the most Texas thing to have happened, so don't worry about it.

Anyway, the outdoor reception had food stations set up all over the property: prime rib, fried chicken, burgers . . . and then I rounded the corner and beheld such a sight. I literally took my shoes off and ran to get my friend Jenny so we could experience it together. We both just stood there and stared at it:

A grilled avocado bar.

What a time to be alive! What a world! We can grill avocados? And treat them like loaded baked potatoes?? Everything is possible now! I believe in miracles!

So grilled avocados became a cherished part of our lives, and Jenny and I became their publicists. We work for free and remain very committed to building their brand.

You can (and should) load these up with sour cream and bacon and cheese and scallions of course, but this—as a base for bruschetta, in place of bread—is one of my favorite ways to serve grilled avocados in the summer.

// First of all, if you aren't already eating bruschetta all summer long, what are you doing with your life? On days when you're not making avocados, brush thick slices of sourdough with olive oil, throw them on the grill, rub one side of each grilled slice with a clove of garlic, and top with this tomato mixture. I would eat that every single day from May to September. But today, because you're about to know about grilled avocados, combine all the topping ingredients ("tomatoes through salt and pepper") in a bowl and stick it in the fridge. This 100% gets better as it sits, so make it a few hours in advance. It's still delicious the next day, of course, but it starts getting a little saturated, so I just give it a couple of hours in the fridge before serving.

// Fire up your grill to medium. (An indoor grill pan would work, too!) Halve each avocado and remove the pit, but don't take the skin off. Brush each avocado half with olive oil and grill facedown for about 3 minutes, rotating them 90 degrees halfway through to get those beautiful grill marks.

// Fill each grilled avocado with the tomato topping, drizzle with balsamic reduction, and sprinkle with that bit of basil you set aside. You eat these right out of the skin with a spoon. Or you can scoop out the flesh, slice it beautifully, and spoon the tomato mix over the top. There are only winners here, no losers. They are adorable and fresh and bright and summery. Send all PR requests to me and Jenny and we will book grilled avocados for your next backyard party.

TOMATO TOPPING

4 ripe farmer-worthy Roma (plum) tomatoes, diced

2 tablespoons olive oil

2 tablespoons balsamic vinegar

2 garlic cloves, diced

⅓ cup chopped fresh basil (reserve a bit for serving)

Juice of ½ lemon

Salt and pepper

—

4 avocados, firm-ish but not hard

Olive oil, for brushing

—

Balsamic Reduction (page 103), for drizzling

Note

On the off chance you have leftover avocados, turn them into grilled guacamole the next day with just some fresh lime juice, chopped white onion, cilantro, and salt.

10

FOOD
THAT COMES
AFTER
YOUR FOOD

YOU GET ONE DESSERT

Crème Brûlée

Crème brûlée. That's it. That's the tweet.

No one comes to me for desserts, so don't act shocked. I don't crave desserts ever, I don't love to bake, and my sweet tooth malfunctioned as a spicy tooth. If I want dessert, I'll have some chips.

However.

My one true sweet love is crème brûlée. I cannot resist it, nor have I ever tried. Nor will I ever try. I know it's just custard with a crunchy sugar crust, but *it is custard with a crunchy sugar crust*. It is my favorite dessert in the entire universe and the singular reason I bought ramekins.

This is what you get in the dessert chapter. If you need additional options, I suggest a bottle of ice-cold champagne. That's it. You've made it to the bottom of my dessert list. But this one recipe is worth its category.

3 cups heavy cream

¼ teaspoon salt

1 vanilla bean, split lengthwise and seeds scraped out (WORTH IT, but if not, use 1 teaspoon vanilla extract)

5 large egg yolks

½ cup sugar, plus another ½ cup or so for topping

// Hello. This is a five-ingredient "fancy" dessert that has never met an enemy. And it is the gift that keeps on giving, because you can (and actually have to) make this early to chill in the fridge, then all you have to do later is broil your sugar crust and serve it like a freaking star.

// At least 5 hours before you want to serve these, preheat your oven to 325°F. Also, put a kettle of water on the stove and bring it to a boil for later.

// In a saucepan, combine the cream, salt, and vanilla seeds (throw the scraped-out pod in there, too) and heat over medium heat until the cream comes to a simmer—do not let it boil. Immediately take it off the heat and let it sit for 5 minutes, then fish out the vanilla bean pod.

// While the cream is cooling, in a medium bowl, whisk together the egg yolks and ½ cup of the sugar until they look butter-yellow and glossy, around 2 minutes. While whisking continuously, slowly pour about a quarter of the warm cream into the egg yolks and whisk until combined. (This is called tempering and you do it so you don't end up with scrambled eggs.) Whisk it all back into the pot with rest of the warm cream so it's smooth and gorgeous.

// Place six broiler-safe 4-ounce ramekins in a roasting pan and fill each one with the custard. (Or use smaller ramekins and end up with more servings!) Carefully fill the pan with enough hot water from the kettle to come 1 inch up the sides of the ramekins. This creates a cozy, warm, humid sauna inside your oven, which allows your crème brûlées to become perfect. Carefully transfer the roasting pan to your oven and bake for 30 minutes-ish. The edges should be set and the middles a little jiggly (the title of my next book, a body memoir). They may need another 5 to 10 minutes, but I start checking at the 25-minute mark. Overcooked crème brûlées are like overcooked steaks: a criminal offense.

RECIPE CONTINUES

// Take them out of their water bath, let them cool completely, then cover and refrigerate for **at least 4 hours** or up to 2 days. Yay! Make-ahead!

// When you're ready to serve them, heat up your broiler, with the top rack 2 to 3 inches from the heat source.

// Place the ramekins on a rimmed baking sheet (or dump the water out of the roasting pan and use that) and sprinkle the tops of the custards with the rest of the sugar, dividing it evenly and covering the tops completely. Slide them under your broiler and watch them like a hawk, dessert maker. You want the sugar melted and browned and bubbling, like the crunchy sugar crust it was born to be; this will take 3 to 5 minutes. (If you're fancy, you could skip the oven and use a kitchen torch to crisp that sugar right up.) *Brûlée* means "burnt," so now you know how it wants to manifest. Get there.

// This is the best dessert in the world. The greatest dinner party flex. The creamiest, lightest, crunchiest, yummiest little scoop of custard heaven. If I ever say I don't want dessert but I'll just have "a bite" of your crème brûlée, do not believe me as far as you can throw me.

There are tons of variations you can try once you master this OG recipe. You can add to the custard:

+ **Lemon**
+ **Cinnamon**
+ **Bananas**
+ **Chocolate**
+ **Nutella**
+ **Espresso**
+ **Pumpkin**

You can top the crème brûlée with:

+ **Berries**
+ **Salted caramel**
+ **Candied ginger**
+ **Candied lemon peel**
+ **Toasted coconut**
+ **Toasted pistachios**

ACKNOWLEDGMENTS

How many people does it take to wrangle a cookbook out of an amateur? All the following folks plus the prayers of the ancestors and all God's angels:

None of us are holding this book without the team at Harvest. These are the most non-risk-averse people in the business. They came in early and hot and said, "We like you. We like this. Give us this cookbook and we swear we will print it." I cannot even describe the patience, enthusiasm, and outrageous levels of expertise they doled out to me. Endless thanks to Anwesha Basu, Deb Brody, Andrea DeWerd, Melissa Lotfy, Rachel Meyers, Karen Murgolo, Jacqueline Quirk, and designer Laura Palese (Women! Women everywhere!), and a very special bear hug to my editor, Stephanie Fletcher, who did it all: she project-managed Jen Hatmaker and for that, she deserves to retire immediately and spend the rest of her days in Tuscany. Thank you, team. You have been an utter delight.

I thought long and hard about this paragraph, because it cannot be reduced to "Thanks to my cookbook photographer, Mackenzie Smith Kelley." M, you were more than that; you were a partner. I wrote all the words, but you and your team brought this book to life. The look, the feel, the fun, the Jen things, the Texas nods—your special brand of magic is all over this project. We made every big decision together. This book is ours. Your team can literally not get enough praise: (Hot) Taylor Cumbie, Matie Aizpurua, Mary McNally, Eric Moreno, Max Puglisi, and lighting wizard (Big) Taylor Jones and son Ty. You made every recipe. You styled every picture. You pulled off not one but two complicated cover shoots. You never stopped smiling. You were a joy to me every single day. Thank you for making this book beautiful beyond all my dreams.

I literally cannot envision my life without my longtime agents, Curtis Yates and Mike Salisbury. Guys, you stick with me through every new iteration. *"A cookbook? Sure! This makes sense! Let's make it happen!"* And you made it happen. You are my champions. Thank you for believing in me. You two are my favorites. I've loved you since Sealy first compared me to a horse.

If it weren't for my assistant, Amanda Duckett, there would be no books, no podcasts, no correspondence, no events, no completed deadlines, and no career. This is not hyperbole. AKD, you are my second brain; really, my first brain and everyone knows it. I cannot believe we are approaching our ten year anni together. You are the most loyal, capable, organized person in my entire life, and you hold a dozen worlds together including mine. I love you almost enough to start using my iCalendar.

If you are reading this, it is because Amy Chandy and her business development squad found a way to get it in your hands. When I say "my team," it is always you. You are my best partners and favorite people, and there is not a single thing I touch that doesn't find lift off under your execution. Nothing. Nada. Anna Trent, Rachel Watkins, Pepper Sweeney, Chelsea Vaughn, Clay Gillespie, Amanda and Ray Garcia: at this point, we have been through it all, and no matter what harebrained idea I come up with, Amy will say "Let's do it!" and you guys will pull it off. I love you, I love you, I love you.

Enormous thanks to my volunteer recipe testers! Y'all jumped into ACTION and without question made this cookbook better. I made who-knows-how-many edits based on your feedback. Happy eaters have you to thank for having the right amount of salt, spice, and peppers since I originally included *too much of everything*. Allegedly.

Who are "these people" to me?

My OG family is the one I would pick if I had a zillion to choose from. Mom, thanks for letting me talk shit about our food in the '80s. Did you boil broccoli into mush? You did, but *that is your business and prerogative*. Fam, I have endless stories to tell in this cookbook because of our weird little life. Between Lindsay's chicken wings, Drew's chicken potpie trauma Mom says he made up, Grandma's carrots, and our shared table for over four decades, there isn't a food memory without you. Add in the people who married us and picked us, and food is our whole family deal. We are the worst and the best, and I love us.

I have fed no people more than the five children that belong to me: Gavin, Sydney, Caleb, Ben, and Remy. You know what? Cooking for you was always fun, because you are enthusiastic, adventurous eaters who will try almost anything. And! You always, always thank me for cooking. Now that I think of it, this is a damn family miracle so I forgive you for *all the other tomfoolery*. I have loved feeding your hungry little mouths for over two decades. You are the greatest loves of my life.

The only people I have eaten with more than my fam are my best friends. I guess the amount of food (and wine) we have cooked and consumed together hovers around the million-ton mark. The endless, endless hours we have gathered around the table is my life's joy. Hell, YOU are my life's joy. Jenny, Shonna, Megan, Trina, and all the husbands: I love you so much, I could die.

And to Tyler who can't eat 80 percent of these recipes because I fell in love with a vegetarian: I will come up with meatless versions for you, although you are out of luck on the beef tenderloin. You had me at fries and honey mustard, baby. I love you. I will photoshop you into these pages. It's like you were always here.

INDEX

"*Feed These People* is the cookbook my family wishes I would write! Written in Jen's encouraging, relaxed, and let's-get-after-it-and-have-some-fun voice, this is the kind of cookbook you turn to time and time again, dirtying the pages as you mark your favorites for years before passing it on to the next deserving—and fun-loving—cook in your family. Jen, you had me at Diner Cheeseburger Sliders with Hot Trash Sauce. And Fried Avocado Tacos with Poblano Ranch. And Crème Brûlée! Jeez. Can you invite me to dinner already?"

—AMANDA HAAS, BESTSELLING COOKBOOK AUTHOR AND
FOUNDER OF HOUSE OF HAAS COOKING SCHOOL

"*Feed These People* is for all of us scattered, hungry home cooks doing our best to trick the ones we love into thinking we're wizards in the kitchen. Jen makes us believe we really can do this thing and gives us the plan. Cackling and connecting and leaving the dishes until morning—this cookbook is a national treasure. I can't wait to make a mess of my copy."

—SHANNAN MARTIN,
AUTHOR OF *START WITH HELLO* AND
THE MINISTRY OF ORDINARY PLACES

"Finally, a cookbook for normals! The recipes are for people craving repeat-worthy, flavor-packed, very extra (without being fussy) meals. So basically, this is a book of magic. Cooking magic! Jen Hatmaker's approach to feeding the people we love is a whole master class in everyday cooking and making your kitchen your own. *Feed These People* has a permanent spot in my kitchen, it is my new go-to book of foods and flavors. And magic."

—BRI McKOY, AUTHOR OF *COME & EAT: A CELEBRATION OF LOVE AND GRACE AROUND THE EVERYDAY TABLE*